FOLLOWING THE LINES

World War II as Experienced by a Belgian Girl

Irène Litz-Barré

Ten|16
PRESS

www.ten16press.com - Waukesha, WI

Following the Lines
World War II as Experienced by a Belgian Girl
Copyrighted © 2017, 2022 Irène Litz-Barré
ISBN 978-1-943331-45-1
First Edition

Following the Lines
World War II as Experienced by a Belgian Girl
by Irène Litz-Barré

For information, please contact:

Ten|16
PRESS

www.ten16press.com
Waukesha, WI

Cover photo property of Irène Litz-Barré
Cover picture is of Réalmont, France, where Irène and her mother spent three months in evacuation.
Cover design by Therese Joanis and Shannon Ishizaki

Why do lines attract my attention? Lines of any kind, straight, crooked or curvy, plunge my mind in positive, secure, nostalgic, or even rebellious moods. Is it the curiosity to see where they lead to or the echo of surmounted rough times and backlashes that some strategic lines pushed me along?

I let you judge and, hopefully, enjoy the printed ones my memories had made me align.

This story is just a guided tour of a war crater inlaid in a growing mind and heart.

To my beloved boys,
my son Michel/Michael
and my grandson Enzo.

Acknowledgements

This memoir was sketched in Zug, Switzerland, and Brussels, Belgium. Some names and dates were verified through the booklet issued from the European Union exhibition in the Musée du Cinquantenaire in Brussels titled *I was Twenty in 1945.*

It was rewritten in slightly better English in Washington D.C., and Milwaukee, Wisconsin, by French-Belgian Walloon on-the-edge, born Irène Barré.

The story finally "buckled up" thanks to convincing Dareene Roisler, tactful Nancy Martin, and the members of the Writing Class at the Alexian Village of Milwaukee. Carolyn Kott Washburne edited my miscreant commas and suggested clarifications.

The "make up" with pictures is due to Michael.

Table of Contents

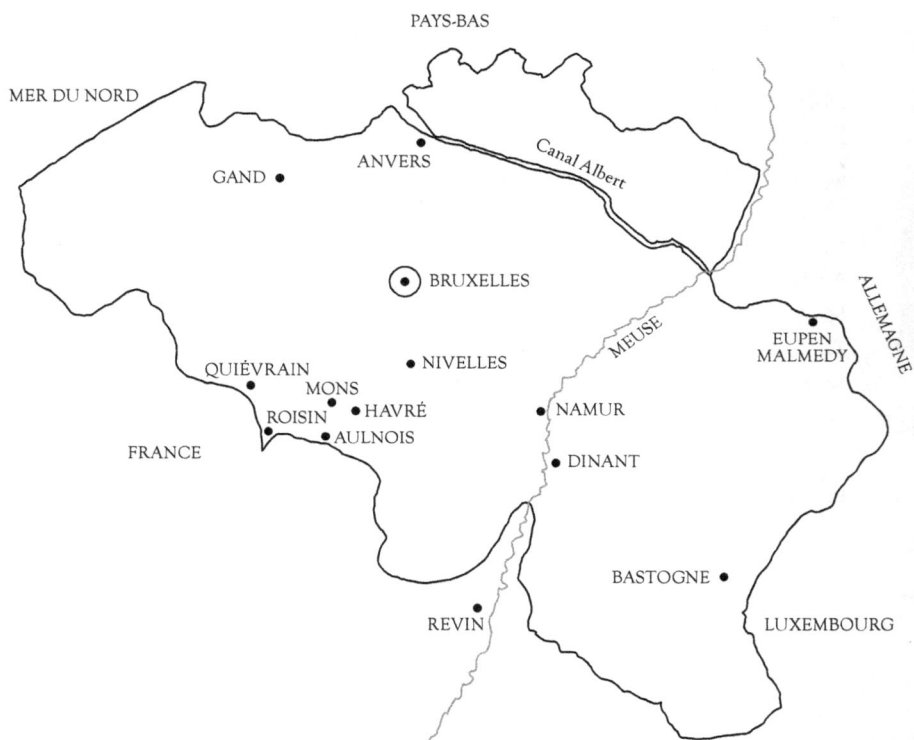

Map of Belgium

CHAPTER ONE
Before The War

French	German	English
Allemagne	- Deutschland	- Germany
Belgique	- Belgien	- Belgium
France	- Frankreich	- France

The three languages represent identity, oppression, and liberation. French is my native language, and I learned some German by necessity. English represents the language of our liberators. Each section starts with a term in all three languages.

Frontière – Grenze – Border

In Belgium, French is spoken in Wallonia, Dutch in the Flanders, German in the Eupen-Malmédy pocket, each with dialects. Roisin, the Walloon village where I grew up, was like a scratch on the French border with straddling houses. Quiet and picturesque it looked like the first page of a storybook. It opened on rolling farmland and a forest. Many of the twelve hundred fifty inhabitants were farmers, brewers, marble cutters, and frontier workers that commuted across the border to French factory jobs. The handful of smugglers' gangs could camouflage under the most conventional professions. At that time, they passed tobacco and alcohol across the border, on foot and with specially trained dogs. Our little village lay like a medal in the sun, on one side shiny smiles and friendship, on the reverse, hidden malevolence.

There was no local newspaper, discretion being a component of security, chiefly among the smugglers. Anyway, sometimes on the street, one could notice a slight move in a curtain, a shutter that could imperceptibly open, showing that not too much could be ignored.

At the end of the 1930s, our village lay just at the foot of an intricate underground stretch of the French Maginot Line. Barely visible from the outside, this fortress had active life and traffic in its two underground floors.

Gendarmerie in Roisin

Then came the war! World War II, with its deep perturbation. Some extremism forced people to be even more secretive but let most of them be heartily helpful, compassionate, and sometimes heroic.

Marcel (Dad), Irène, Maman (Jeanne), Aunt Irène (mom's sister) and Uncle Marcel in 1933

Famille – Familie – Family

On our side, my father was the officer commander of the Belgian gendarmerie's station, Adjudant Chef Marcel Barré. The Gendarmerie Corps, which has now disappeared, was a mixture of army and police. My father's brigade oversaw seven villages. Befitting his future, Dad was born in France of Belgian parents. Dad was an Ardennais, a prototype of the inhabitants from the French-speaking part of Belgium covered with forests: clear complexion, dark brown curly hair, and blue eyes that could see "through" to the hidden truth. He was friendly to everyone, but knew what was really going on. Energetic but nevertheless affable, part of his philosophy was to disarm with a smile. Not especially devoted to military rigidity, he was the right man to face the inevitable diplomatic thorns of a life on the border.

My active mother, Jeanne Lambert, from a more industrial part of the French speaking Belgium, had the Walloon roots with the addition of her mother's inexplicable Flemish family name, Victorine Vandenscrick. Maman had a fair matte complexion, light brown thick hair, and grayish blue eyes. She was a generous lady who naturally succeeded in every task she touched, practical or artistic. I appreciated her creativity, excellent cooking and knitting.

Myself, I am Irène Barré (nicknames Nénette or Chon-chon), a moderate tomboy, with dark thick wavy hair and blue eyes. I liked the nickname Nénette given me by my grandmother. Chon-Chon, a pet name I earned playing in a coal bin, means piggie. I attended school in the village for three years and, as a third grader, started to commute to the Sainte Marie School in Quiévrain, a city ten miles away, but still on the border.

Vie – Lebenslauf – Life
We lived in the official building, all bricks, stones and high ceilings. It was located at the edge of a closed park that had previously been partly used as a paddock when the gendarmerie had horses on duty. A few years before our arrival, the horses had been, for the sake of modernity, modernly, replaced by bicycles. The paddock had been adorned with

locusts, linden trees, lilacs, and flower beds around a large lawn. Some paths opened on long, private gardens. The empty stables were partly reserved for the maintenance and to the big dogs: Max the German shepherd and Rip the black Bouvier des Flandres,

Rip, the strongest puppy with careful Irène

who, in spite of their environment and their taming, could not stand the postman's uniform. The dogs rushed the gate, teethed barred, growling every day to greet the postman.

Four other gendarmes' families lived on the grounds. The children were teens by degrees: three boys, one girl, followed by a trio of toddlers. A bit isolated because of the north edge location and the villagers' cautious disposition, the kids formed a condensed mini-society. At times Paul, the oldest boy, engineered the games, Marco the second, assured the peace and my protection. Odon, the third, played the squirrel part. And I, the youngest, followed as an enthusiast co-partner. The toddlers, Maurice, Jacqueline, and Yvette, gently attracted a sympathetic interest without participating in the games. The police dogs were not partners either. Sometimes Gilbert, the closest farmers' son, joined us and added some of his witty, down-to-earth humor. Everybody was happy in his or her own world.

Espoir – Hoffnung – Hope

Then came the summer of 1939. For a while a political mess was going on, a constant crisscross of plenipotentiary personalities. War? No war?

In spite of being a neutral country, Belgium had some twenty-six-year-old remembrances of the Big War (World War I), which gave some reasons to worry. In August, the pact between Russia and Germany was signed. Right after Poland was invaded. After a few German naval battles, the United Kingdom and France declared war on Germany. Our neutral Belgium closed its borders.

Inqiétude – Angst – Worry

We were immediately concerned, as my father's family lived in France. My grandparents had to shorten the vacations they were spending with us. A very sad good-bye with so many unsettled questions.

Then started the period called "la drôle de guerre" ("the phony war"). Neutral Belgium put its borders under heavy control. A load of inexperienced auxiliaries came to help. The emptied-out stables were equipped for the new men to be quartered. To everyone's disappointment, the police dogs, Max and Rip, had to leave. A farmer living far from our place offered to take Rip. Strange choice, as Rip could not stand any chicken or rabbit—it used to just take him just one quick bite to keep them permanently quiet! Anyway, Rip became a part of the farming system. He learned how to safely carry the cans of milk the farmer put on a carriage after he had milked the cows in the meadow. Perfect, except many months later, when my father had to pass at quite a distance from where the dog was on duty. Rip recognized Dad and leaped over the fence to greet him, caring neither of the carriage nor the cans!

Max went to be a member of his master's family. I guess he missed his partner, Rip, who could set him free after carefully untying his collar with some precise moves and strong teeth.

In our community, optimism was the rule, in spite of a screaming Adolph Hitler scaring us to death on the radio. No wonder the German language stayed stuck in my throat for a long time. All the hustle, our beautiful park and gardens converted into mock battlefields. The gendarmes' exercises and maneuvers and the camp kitchen were quite exciting for the kids. Our brains captured every detail. We memorized their strategic orders. We also repeated the ditties the men sang, rarely with our parents' approval.

All that excitement and the lack of some French

pupils blocked on the other side of the border were not enough to keep us out of school, but paying attention was nearly impossible. I remember the third of September 1939, the closing day of the borders. The panic on the school grounds had been quickly calmed by two paternal gendarmes who come to reassure the foreigners and bring them back into their now-at-war-territory. A regular passage was soon organized for some school kids and recognized frontier workers.

Souvenir – Erinnerung – Remembrance

Armistice Day on November 11, 1939, was drowned in the deepest fog we ever saw. The ceremony at the memorial monument took place anyway; it was an uneasy situation, as we heard the French tanks loudly maneuvering a few miles away. The mixed-up sounds of the engines and the metallic treads blended together in a heavy, ominous noise that penetrated the fog. What was their intention? Were they ready for a "protective" invasion?

Espionage – Spionage – Spying

Another rush of adrenaline came the day a man, dressed like a priest, limping, walking with two canes like an unfortunate vagrant, was arrested at the border. He explained he was trying to join part of his family in France after he had been thrown out of Germany by the Nazis. Maybe? A few cups of coffee and more questions later, my father noticed something was written on the man's cuff, sort of a map. When he realized he was caught, the guy threw his canes away, stood up straight, and arrogantly said, "I am a German officer." His ear heard close by the whiz of my father's iron ruler, which ended up in the office door, breaking it in two. My father's "ruler" was a 16-inch long, half-inch square iron bar. The next noise was the click of handcuffs.

Progressively, people became nervous suspecting any passerby to be a possible member of the fifth column, the name of the German infiltrating organization. On some walls, you could now see posters inviting every citizen to a maximum of attention and discretion. Les oreilles ennemies vous écoutent (The enemy's ears are listening), that poster was illustrated with a very large ear.

So went the ups and downs until the tenth of May 1940.

My father's desk items with the door breaker ruler

Chapter Two
The War Is On

Guerre – Krieg – War

Around four o'clock in the morning of that clear and beautiful day, we were awakened by the noise of a French and a German plane engaged in dogfight for at least for half an hour over the French territory. Then the French plane came down in flames. One of its occupants was able to use his parachute. Here, in our pajamas, we were petrified. For the first time we were witnesses to a real battle with real victims. When the German plane used our neutral Belgian sky to go back home, my father said, "That's it!"

At the same moment, the telephone rang to give the official information: Belgium was invaded, as were Luxembourg and The Netherlands. The general mobilization started. That was followed by the order given to the young men from sixteen to eighteen to leave the country and meet "somewhere in France." They would know later where to be reassembled and trained. The reserve army had to join the active, immediately. Almost every family was concerned. Dad knew we were in the line of fire because of the close-by Maginot Line. So the departure of all the civilians had to be considered.

At that time, the supposedly well-equipped French army on our side and the super-equipped British Empire army on the sea side were coming to help. The first French group that crossed our village was a Special Division on their beautiful Arab horses, followed by inappropriate carriages that looked like farmer's flatbed wagons. On one of them, a soldier was half lying down with a bloody bandage around the head. Dad's disillusioned short comment, "We are cooked."

In the late afternoon, the cities around us were bombed. Quiévrain where I was going to school and Mons in Belgium; Valenciennes, Bavay, and Maubeuge in France, all bombed at the same time. Our house trembled on its foundations. These bombings left hundreds of victims. The next morning we learned that in Quiévrain, among the thirty-nine victims we knew, were two classmates. Gérard, a friend's son, killed at home. Jacques, a colleague in the Latin class, lost a leg. He survived, but his mother was still under the wreckage of their home. Schools closed, traffic, living, and planning largely perturbed, we couldn't have any direct contact with the concerned families. Disturbingly, it took over three months before we could get in touch with everyone.

Like all the other children, my innocent, unconcerned sense of security and my infancy were over. I was a trimester old twelve and a page was definitely turned.

Abandonner – Verlassen – Forsaken

The civilians' evacuation started the next day. Some people were arriving from the German border. They had been pushed to and fro by bombings and military convoys. The French border office was overloaded. Anxiety and fair play were not always pairing well.

A supposed British envoy emerged from an unexpected long foreign embassy car bitterly complaining, offended by not having the supremacy of a preferential passage. Shortly interrupted by shooting from a plunging Stuka dive bomber, he then vindictively attacked my father: "Why didn't you use your gun to shoot the plane? We are poorly defended, and more."

Stuka - still frighening

Apparently that person knew what had to be done. Did I tell you Dad could be impatient? Coldly, Dad came to the car, in accordance with protocol; he asked why the man didn't have an official document to justify his presence on this subsidiary road. Then he said that tickling a surveying Stuka with a handgun would provoke a disastrous machine gun response and added "Your Excellency would help our invaded territory by using his knowledge here rather than fleeing."

Turning to the driver, Dad said: "You are heading in the wrong direction." Then Dad went back to other concerns. Was it really the British ambassador or a priggish bully in this official car? It didn't matter at this frightening time. On the spur of the moment, the noise of a new bombing let the complainer, his wife, and driver accept an unexpected sheltering in our cellar. No ill feelings.

Partir – Abfahren – Leave

Grandma Catherine was with us, on convalescence after a severe attack of rheumatism, and she couldn't walk. We contacted Grandpa in their home in Havré, Belgium. We proposed to him to join us in case of a departure. Could you imagine Grandpa Arnold, a cabinet maker, far from his workshop, his valuable reserve of precious wood? NO WAY! Granpa's ébénistrie workshop kept a large stockpile fine woods aging for him and his carvers to use on inlay projects. Same answer from Aunt Germaine, who would not picture a hazardous and dangerous trip with four young children.

"I would not move even if a German soldier was on

Maternal grandparents Arnold and
Catherine (Victorine)

my chimney" was her comment.

We sure didn't like the idea of going away either. However, we lived in a government building in front of the Maginot Line where shooting could start at any time, so we knew that the order could rapidly come.

Empirer – Schlimmer Werden – To get worse

The Army was doing its best on the Canal Albert, fortifying the first natural barrier near the border. The well-organized enemy seemed to show up everywhere at the same time. The whirlpool of confusing attacks turned madly around our soldiers.

On the thirteenth of May, in the Netherlands, Queen Wilhelmina left the country. The next day twenty-five thousand houses were bombed in Rotterdam. The Dutch surrender was decided on May fifteenth.

Here in Belgium, on the sixteenth came the order to leave the building immediately. Dad had to join his regiment of "Chasseurs Ardennais" in Tournai. Stressful moments. Just before he left I gave him my treasure: a tiny statue of Saint Benoît in a tiny golden case I had received while visiting the abbey of Maredsous with the school. I'll never forget the intense look in his eyes! He told me: "Don't worry, with him, I'll be back soon to Maman and you too."

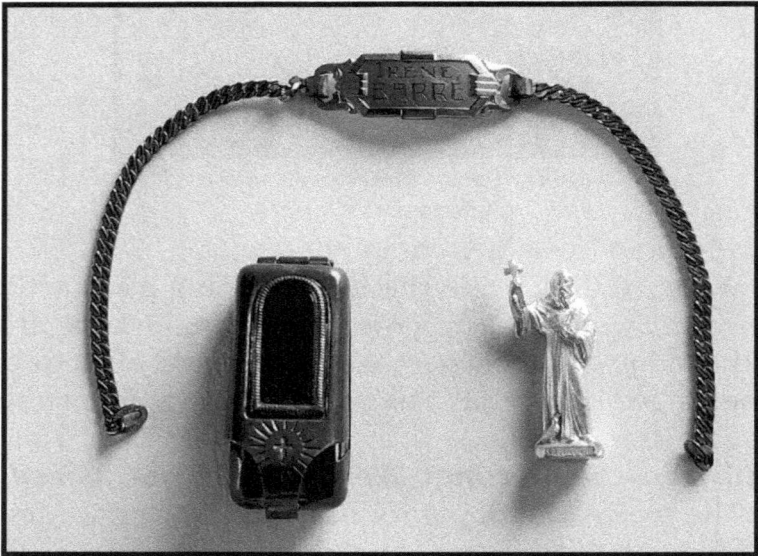

Saint Benoît our busy protector - figure and case
with my braclet

Evacuer – Raumen – Clear

One hour later, Aunt Irène and three-and-a-half-year-old Michel, who came to get the last news, were packed with us. So were the wife of a newcomer gendarme and her daughter Yvette, the director of the primary school and her little boy Emile, some friends and acquaintances, all of us in the last army-requisitioned truck, a coal truck. We were ten officially evacuated, plus the chauffeur, but it was inconceivable not to fill the truck. Total: twenty-six. Impossible to inform my Uncle Marcel who, miraculously, arrived while we were stopped at the border to show THE official paper my father had prepared with all the stamps he had on his desk and the recommendation of a French officer to let us cross the famous line. Uncle Marcel and his bike were dragged on the truck, and so started the twenty-seven of us for a perilous tour.

Not only was I shocked by the events, but to see my uncle, a school director, with tears rolling down his cheeks was puzzling and scary for me. Was our situation so desperate? Well, his eighty-year-old grandmother was visiting, and he had left her at his home thinking he would be gone just a short time. Now, how to let her know that nobody would come back? Who would be able to immediately take care of her, to reassure her?

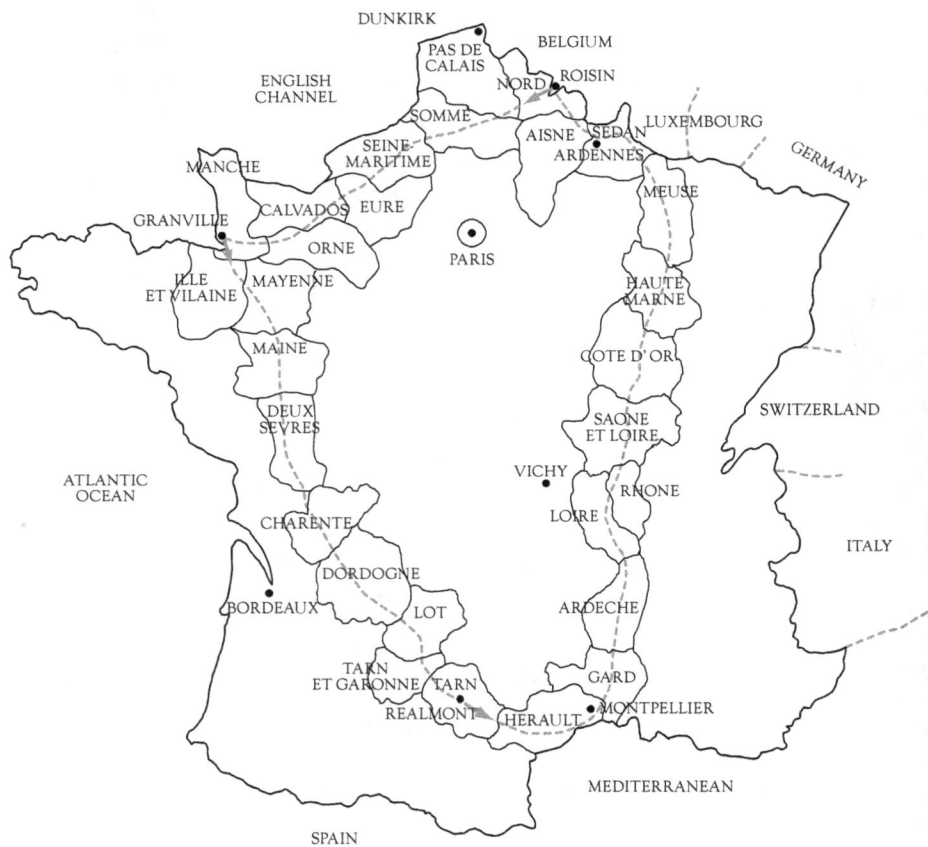

French Evacuation Map

CHAPTER THREE

Evacuation

Emigrant – Auswanderer – Emigrant

The first day of the trip was like a confusing nightmare. No one could find a conversation able to be followed. Conversations went unfinished and attentions were elsewhere. When it came time to find a night shelter, we were in the surroundings of Cambrai, France. Noticing a large farm, the chauffeur thought we could ask there for some help. Before we even came to a complete stop, we knew we were not welcome. A furious lady swooped out, like a screaming harpy eagle, insulting us. When that harpy saw our Belgian license plate, she called us vagrants, people who could not stop the Germans, beggars, and more. Abashed, the Club 27 stayed silent. Then my sweet Grandma's voice clearly came out, "We are coming from an invaded neutral country, Madame. You don't seem to know much about what happened, but by tomorrow you'll be able to return all of your complements on yourself. I wish you good luck." The truck driver moved on.

We were lucky enough to have survived the Stuka's attacks and pass through the cities before the heavy bombings.

Oasis – Oase – Oasis

Part of our French family had already been evacuated on the Normandy coast with the École Normale. My cousin Marguerite was teaching at the very respected teachers' college. Her Aunt Boka and her mother were with her. Her mother, Aunt Victoria, was my idol aunt. Distinguished, she was always attentive to everyone. She had been the first woman admitted to teach sciences in a college. Her father, dear Uncle Ernest, had died the year before. They were now in Granville, on the south of this channel coast, a pleasant city on a cliff, and they were our rallying point. It took us four days to cover the three hundred miles to Granville.

Imagine their surprise when, from their balcony, among the flood of refugees, they recognized us. My refined Aunt Victoria screamed "Jeanne!" when they saw our peculiar group in a coal truck with my mother standing up—her hat on—at that time, ladies didn't go hatless. We were trying to find their Hôtel d'Angleterre. How reassured were we to find beloved ones in a safe place.

*Cousin Marguerite, professor at the
Ecole Normale in Douai, France*

*Aunt Victoria, the first lady
to teach Sciences in a college*

*Aunt Boka, their Douais' home
affective and effective intendant*

Journal de bord – Reisebuch – Logbook

They were anxious to know what we had gone through. After we had exchanged news and put our wits together, we could talk about Dad leaving for the front and the loss of common friends and acquaintances in the bombings. We described our dramatic departure on a shortcut through the Maginot Line. We sure didn't forget the Stuka's attacks, which had forced us, a few times, to jump into ditches, leaving Grandma stuck in her chair on the truck. She didn't want us to lose any time with her, so, as protection, we just dropped on her the mattress my cautious mother had taken along.

We also mentioned the anecdote of the lady, who, later on, on the main road, totally panicked by the plunging plane's roar, screamed her local incantation: "Saint Expedit, expedite the bomb further away!" Sort of a local, self-protective prayer for the incredibly long line of refugees that moved slowly by car, carriage, on bike, even on foot. It became a lifelong memory about strafing Stukas. I still shiver when I see them on a screen. I keep clearly hearing their bullets' impact in the grass ditches.

Stuka - frightening even on a stamp

Aide – Hilfe – Help

We felt blessed for the help on our way. The two teachers on board went to schools and asked for a roof for the night. This was not so simple, as Grandma and her chair formed an inseparable couple. Of course, the Club 27 had to split up, but every time, the guest rooms were opened for us, and we were offered dinner and a copious breakfast. What compassionate people!

The first night, after the Cambrai's "harpy eagle's hit," the only one we met on our long way, we were still in the north, in Fins. An old couple who lived in a cottage surrounded by a flowery garden treated us like family members.

The second night, in Triechateau, we stayed in a very modern school. The director, whose husband was on the front line, received us warmly.

The third night we were in Normandy, in Duranville, in a tiny house with a thatched roof. Our hostess had a heart equal to her imposing corpulence. There we heard a tragicomic story. A couple who was the last to leave their village was ready to go when they discovered an old aunt—dead.

It was impossible then to find an immediate solution to the problem, so they rolled her in their best carpet, pushed her on the roof of their car, and away they went. Later on, exhausted, they stopped to rest for a while. When ready to drive again, surprise, the carpet had disappeared. Years later we heard that it took this poor couple over twenty years of formalities to turn this disappearance into an official death. For now, imagine the thieves' faces when they discovered the contents.

Now we happily were in Granville—SAFE. Aunt

Victoria was hoping we could stay together until the end of the war, and so did our family. The next morning we had to register at the City Hall. There specific plans had been made: the people from every city in danger of attack were assigned to a safe place.

Since October, Granville had already sheltered Douai's École Normale and high schools. As the situation was getting worse (Germans had entered Cambrai), the city now awaited the rest of the Douai's population. So the Belgian citizens had to reach Toulouse, where they would be reassembled. It was not next door. Over five hundred more miles to cover. Sadly we left our refuge. Too bad we obeyed too promptly. The following night, all the railway traffic was blocked by bombing, and the expected arrivals never made it.

Voyage – Reise – Journey

Here we were, on the road again, heading south. Some planes still came to check our procession, but there was no more shooting. We had four more wandering days. As time passed, we adopted sort of a Gypsy style, laundry floating in the wind. Laundry roughly washed when water, security, and possible privacy were available. We used the same strategy to satisfy natural needs. It was better to get organized before the morning departure. A stop depended on the events, the traffic, and, the driver's own schedule. He wanted to keep going to maintain his schedule.

On the truck, to be protected from wind, people wrapped themselves in blankets or whatever was on hand. I wore a bonnet-style, Snoopy WWI pilot cap. Even Maman replaced her hat with a shawl. I noticed another change in my lively mother. She was now taking everybody under her wing with calm and efficiency. Poor Maman. Because she carried the only official paper in our possession, in the big cities we passed through, she had to line up at the prefecture for the new gas ration coupons.

Secretly, while waiting in the truck with Grandma, I worried that a sudden change would separate us. Most of the other passengers were taking some exercise.

Once my feeling about my uncle's perfection was solidly chipped when he came back holding little Michel on his arm, little Michel licking an enormous ice-cream. Where could they have found that treasure, and bought nothing for thirsty Grandma and me?

Possible restaurants for travelers were all closed. The few open had a very limited menu, mostly soups. All variety of food were unavailable – butchers, bakeries, and green groceries all closed. We never ate so many hard boiled eggs; they were easy to find, boil, and take away. Still a lot of goodhearted people came at the light stops to offer us fruits, canned food, and drinks. From Angers, on the Loire River, I still have in mind and heart a little older lady who was abashed by the situation. She seemed so distressed to not be able to offer more than the cans of sardines she had obviously snapped from her pantry.

The first night we arrived in Pont-de-Cé. This time the teachers' tactic didn't work, as there was no school in this remote little place. A farmer family sheltered us. As the truck could not stay on the road, they suggested emptying a barn. The men went to clear out grape-harvesters' material and the local hearse.

A good night anyway. The next morning the generous hostess prepared a huge picnic basket for which we were thankful the whole day long.

After General Rommel's passage in Cambrai, the big tanks, the Panzers, entered Abbeville. The adults did not emphasize the problems, as there were five kids on board: two almost four years old, two twelve (myself and a new girl), and the driver's son a, "old" fourteen. They tried to attract our attention to the change of countryside, the rivers we crossed. Each one of us stayed close to his own people "just in case." We were like puppies—our ears picked up even the most discreet whisper. Our instinctive way of absorbing feelings told us that tourism could not have become the main purpose of this adventure. On top of that, our name, address and "pedigree" hanging around our neck. A paper tag listed our name, home address and health details in a protective sleeve hung by a cord, even at night. Parents always with the insistent warning "Don't take it off, don't lose it." All this and more kept us far from relaxation.

One night we found a teacher in Morgon, a young girl who lived with her grandfather. Worried about our disturbed diet, in spite of a stormy rain, they rushed to their garden, picked fast-cooking veggies, and made the most delicious soup with sorrel, cream and egg yolks, followed by an enormous salad with small chunks of bread. No more loaves, no more meat, as both baker and butcher were on the front line. We enjoyed the last of the supplies from home, most appreciated the rest of the chunk of dried, smoked ham Maman had packed just before we had left home. Dear smoked ham, which had already been mostly consumed with our Club 27 "companions of misery.

The Panzer tanks kept going on their open road to the sea; at least they were not following us anymore. The traffic had become as heavy as possible. French residents from the North were joining us now, which aggravated the space, gas, and food problems. These questions were the adults' concern. A sky empty of warlike planes had brought some peace to our minds, enough to notice that the houses had a different style, less and less bricks. The roofs were covered with roman round tiles. Their color also was different, as was the smell of trees and flowers that didn't grow in our area.

The following night we slept in Cressensac at a grocery store. There was some restriction in the food distribution, but the compassionate grocer made us pick some extras.

The next morning the news came that Toulouse, our destination, was buried under thousands of refugees spread all over the city and surroundings. They temporarily lived in their cars while waiting for a decent place. The rising heat was no help either, temperatures above 30° Celsius was hot for springtime. Officials advised us to head in the direction of Salvagnac in the Department of the Tarn. That put us deeper into that southern part of France. Because of the hunt for gas coupons, the driver had to cross overcrowded cities. With the traffic, the unusual heat, and the fatigue, he took a wrong turn.

Chance – Glück – Luck

Because of that mistake, at night we ended up in Réalmont instead of Salvagnac, but still in the same Tarn Department. In spite of the late hour, the teachers' strategy fortunately worked again. The family found a place at the boys' school, welcomed by Mrs. Cosne, whose husband was an officer at the front line on the Somme. Her parents, evacuated from Moulins, were with her. Maman and I stayed at the girls' school with Miss Moret and her parents.

We arrived physically and emotionally exhausted. Wonderful people. Not only did they show deep sympathy, but they provided dinner, a bedroom, and the most enjoyable bath I can remember, a warm bath perfumed with lavender and lemon.

The next morning they advised us to inquire at the City Hall. Réalmont wasn't waiting for official refugees. We were the first ones. Maybe they would arrange for us to stay there. That they fortunately did.

CHAPTER FOUR

Shelter

Accueil – Willkommen – Welcome

Hurray! There were a few empty houses and apartments in the city that would charitably take care of the rent. Among their first refugees, they gave our Club 27 the choice of available free housing. For us, we picked a very old house, a little bit out of the center. It had a ground floor where Grandma could get around. It was located at the edge of a large garden. The local gardener Dominique was the owner, and he had been using that house for tool storage for over twenty years. We only had one neighbor, a widow named Marie. Her son, Honoré, was the city carpenter. With his wife, Anna, and the four grandchildren, they visited Marie every day. Everybody came to empty the place of pots, tools, plants, spiders (no hearse there). They just forgot a couple of rats.

Our hostess, Miss Moret, kept us until the house was ready to be occupied. There were still some pieces of furniture inside. The city provided a few chairs and a wood-burning stove that got squeezed in the large chimney. Under the staircase was enough room to put a bed for Grandma—a bit squeaky (the bed, not Grandma). In a very large room on the second floor, each of us had a summer camp-style bed. It took a lot of imagination to make the room suitable for five.

Uncle Marcel reinforced the chimney opening, fearing a visit from the escaped rats.

More good-hearted people brought plates, cups, glasses, pots, and pans. For the water, we had a drain in the kitchen, but no running water. For water refills we had to go outside to the pump. Charitable Marie let us use her well plus the access to two large, outdoor stone basins for laundry washing. You don't waste natural fertilizer, so the body "emptying" was done in the next vineyard. A chamber pot was necessary at night and those were also emptied in the vineyard. To isolate the pot or take a mock shower in the attic near the room needed some tactics. "Please bring: chair, large bucket, water, sponge, soap, and towel" Maman would say, all the while looking for where the undesirable rats were hiding.

We felt like we had landed on another planet, but the six of us were still together in one piece and healthy. We had nice people around, and we could even provide an address that we pompously titled "Villa Dominique on Roquecourbe Road." Roquecourbe was a city about ten miles away on the curvy road behind the high hill.

Not so many questions marks anymore, although still some serious ones: how long would we live here? And how?

The first thing to do was to give our address to Aunt Victoria, our rallying point in Granville, hoping she would receive it soon. The mail then was like a balloon in the wind.

We expected many messages from family and friends. I wasn't worried for my father; you remember he was under serious protection—so were we, obviously. Anyway, some news from him would have been the most welcomed, chiefly since I had the impression my family wasn't totally sharing my certainty.

Many refugees, like waves, arrived downtown. According to which side the news came from, the fighting situation was under control or everything was burning.

Ecole – Schule – School

To get my mind out of this chaos, good Miss Moret took me in her class. I would be considered a visitor because our school programs were so different. The kids were nice, used to welcoming and accepting exotic birds, since they already had a few Spaniards who had flown away from the 1936 civil war in their country.

I was amazed by the gray overall smocks they wore covering their clothes. Amazed by the rapidity of their speech, by their accent. Their accent! As sunny as their region. They enunciated every letter like the Italians, so the spelling was easier that way. With the local children, I studied French geography, history and picked up their regional notation of the French language. We learned a folklore song in the quaint local Occitan language. Different too, the way they said "bonsoir"—good evening—right after 12 a.m. and "adieu" instead of au revoir—good-bye. I enjoyed every minute at school. Back home, I talked everyone's ears off with my discoveries and played with Michel, drawing and making him some toys, as many as the available cardboard permitted.

Différence – Verschiedenheit – Difference

After dinner, we adopted the local tradition to sit on the stone bench in front of Marie's house with her and her family. The stones, which had absorbed the sun the all day long, gave off a great scent so unusual for us. The heat coming out of them made the place very pleasant. The house was on the road to the Dadou River. We chatted with the walkers heading to the evening coolness.

Marie had three barely teenage grandchildren: Jacqueline, Gilbert, and Josette, and the adorable and adored Lisou, who was two. A bunch of fun. They were as agile as squirrels, except Josette, who suffered from a heart malformation. Her siblings cautiously pushed her wheelchair, but at the top of the street, they could not resist letting her go. Josette loved it; she always arrived safely in loud giggles covering up her Grandma's high-pitched screams. We didn't play too much, but talked, talked to exhaustion, curious to know how life was in Belgium and here. So many questions!

South: "How can you manage without olive oil, fresh almonds, fresh figs, sourdough bread, and wine?"

North: "How can you manage without gingerbread, sugar roots, yeast bread, beer, and butter?

Gilbert deepened his inquiry, "Butter? With what do you eat butter?"

"Well, we eat butter on bread, on pancakes, on baked potatoes, in sauces."

Completely astonished at the volume of butter ingested, Gilbert had this memorable comment: "Then you must shit all yellow." I told you they were funny.

Jacqueline and her brother,
the 'troubled by butter' Gilbert

The differences were not only gastronomical. Following the southern schedule, as the school started at 9 a.m., we could enjoy the cool evenings and avoid going to bed before ten o'clock. What a pleasant change. When ready to go home, the kids sung this strange lullaby: "May all the fleas, have a big feast in your bed." Sometimes the fleas obeyed. After lights out, we went to sleep, lulled by toad croaking and dozens of crickets and cicadas buzzing.

Relaxing evenings before the black day of May 28.

Tournant – Wendepunkt – Watershed

After eighteen days of terrible battles, the Belgian Army had reached the point of complete disintegration.

King Léopold III, after contacting the Allies and then his government, decided to surrender. The government left for Bordeaux in southwest France, and the King stayed in Belgium as a war prisoner.

Etranger – Fremde – Foreigner

Here, frantically beating his drum, with a cavernous voice, the old-style town crier brought the news. CONSTERNATION. An icy shower. Soon after, some bad-minded people concluded that the King, the Belgians, and us, as a consequence, were an untrustworthy bunch responsible for the defeat. Guess they were thinking about camps for us. The situation wasn't easy for a few days until it was made clear that: Most obviously former neutral Belgium didn't have as many men as its Allies.

That starting from May 12, the King had followed the French General Gamelin's directions.

That the famous Maginot Line hadn't totally worked out, as the Germans had turned around it when unexpectedly coming from the region of Sedan.

That, on the 26th, the British troops had given up and decided to go back home.

So instead of being "new German" we became more or less excess stateless persons.

Even us, the children, got involved in the whirlpool; we asked how and why more often. Could we ever go back to Belgium, would we see our people again, would we receive news from them? Nothing had yet come from Granville. Now, in this situation, where was my father?

Où? – Wo? – Where?

The tension was high among the anxious refugees. Practical life was starting to become difficult, as the banking system was upside down. The French government helped by giving ten francs a day for an adult and six for a child. I presumed it was not too much. Fortunately, we bought our veggies from our kind landlord Dominique, who didn't charge the store price and always left a little extra for the "pitchouns" (the kids). Maman managed to keep the pot boiling and always served good meals, for she was an inventive cook. Poor Maman. I often saw her sweating in front of the wood-burning stove. She also tried hard to make the old furniture and the red tile covered floor look better and lose the musty smell of their inactivity. She took care of Grandma who, thanks to the dry climate, felt much better.

Children have antennas. I could feel Maman's anxiety, and sometimes I caught tears in her eyes. Then, hidden in my corner, I felt miserable trying to find an appropriate diversion and not ask questions that could amplify her worries. Thank God, our loving and understanding Grandma was with us. My aunt took good care of her lively and lovely little boy, but she sounded so depressed. My uncle seemed to be preoccupied by the provision of burning wood he had to find in the forest and then meticulously cut in absolutely regular pieces. Guess it was a way to convince himself that things could still be done right.

The world was turning anyway. The evenings on the bench kept going on; they calmed down the agitation of the days. The heat stayed high at night. There was one very noisy nighttime thunderstorm; there was so much lightning we could see outside like in the daytime. The wind was blowing so badly that, in the meadow in front of our house, an enormous haystack got blown up in the air and disappeared. Scary! This was followed by the most welcomed rain in this dry region. The next morning the sky was crystal clear and the soil stone dry again.

Organiser – Organisieren – Organize

As our stopover seemed to become rather unlimited, some changes were necessary. We forgot about the northern habits and became more considerate of the southern ones: Don't take the sun as a present, hide from it, protect your skin, wear a hat, the outside heat because of the burning sun was to be kept shuttered out, inside coolness because of deep house foundations and thick stone walls was to be kept shut inside with window shutters drawn. As poorly equipped as we were, keeping the food safe was a performance. Marie let us use her cool cellar carved in the rock. We had to change our diet going from butter to oil—to Gilbert's relief. Anyway, kind Dr. Aussenac, the family doctor, came a few times to medically stop unpleasant diarrhea episodes.

The first mail from Granville arrived on June 1. A short message: they were fine. It also contained a postcard from a friend's husband. Nothing else for others. What a disappointment.

The city did its best to organize for an uncertain future. Many refugees previously stuck in Toulouse were spreading around. We were now twelve hundred who came from everywhere.

Routine – Routine – Routine

The opening of a Belgian school was decided upon, as there were a few teachers around. Not my primary school director uncle, busy as you know. I didn't think too much about that push back into the routine. I enjoyed the French classes. On top of that, that new school was a fifteen minute walk away from home and, even if paper and pencils could be provided, we had no adequate books to cover the program. It was more to keep us busy than to seriously educate us.

As the Belgian academic authorities could not imagine a change in their traditional schedule, we started at eight, came back for lunch at 11:30, went back at 1:30 until four, which means that, for the lunch break, we were the only nuts on the street. The locals were taking a nap; their schools started later. Even cats and dogs avoided the peak heat. One day an old lady, typically dressed in black, her large straw hat on, called me from her window.

"My poor 'pitchounette,' where are you going at this time of day?"

"To the Belgian school Ma'am."

Her eyes looked up to heaven and she said, "These Belgians are completely "fada" (crazy)."

Sweating, I totally agreed with her. I felt that I fitted into their informal, flexible, and intelligent southern system. My secret hope was to see my father arriving on his bike, sure he would like it too and we would stay HERE. The only plus I childishly appreciated was the new overall Maman bought me at the nice boutique still carrying some colorful cotton material, which I considered as a novelty. Bye-bye the traditional black school outfit. It was a bit large, but I will grow.

Incertitude – Ungewissheit – Uncertainty

Our social life was limited. The other displaced people we met out of our circle were worried about the heat getting higher, like the prices; the sugar rationing had turned to one monthly pound per person, and anything not locally produced harder and harder to find. When the war situation came into the conversation, the weariness could reach its peak. Parents and children alike worried about what would happen next.

The French minister Paul Raynaud's speeches wanted to be reassuring, while he pleaded for American help. The United States still resisted entering the war. The Germans kept going on.

And now Mussolini was menacing, but his menaces, screamed in Italian, didn't sound as bad as the German ones.

Recommencer – Wieder anfangen – To start again

Anyway, our family life was busy. We took long walks, amazed to see the farmers who worked in their fields with two huge slow oxen attached by a yoke and dragging a plow. We bathed in the nearby Dadou River and picked different kinds of sweet, ripe berries in the forest. Once we climbed the moderately high Mont Caylou, from where we could see the Black Mountain, the far- away summit of the Cévennes' massif.

Good news: after many tremendous efforts, which gained our admiration, Grandma could walk again, still with difficulty, but she could move around. Other news from the family? None. Where are they? Where is Dad?

Every day shopping downtown took a while. I loved

the atmosphere of the bakery and the scent of the grocery store furnished with dark wood. One large wall was entirely covered with little drawers, which diffused the spices' fragrance. I liked the color of the oil in the huge glass container on a counter, chiefly the thousands of tiny bubbles moving up and down when Miss Ségur pumped out a bottle filling. Peculiar Miss Ségur, an old spinster who, to me, looked like a prune—dark and dry. She was very proud of the variety she offered, and she even had butter, enough to cover a Belgian breakfast. She could not stand indecision. If a customer was lost, gazing at the containers of products in bulk, she would sharply ask, "So, you take some or you don't?" Aside from that impatience, she was nice.

Nouvelles – Nachrichten – News

Succinct messages came through Granville. One was from Aunt Madeleine who had reached her cousins' place in Nevers with her five-year-old daughter, Colette, her mother, and two aunts in their eighties— Arsenic and Old Lace types. My grandparents and Uncle Charles had ended up in Vendée, in Les-Sables d' Olonne, where they lived with a fisherman's family. They were doing fine too. Seven of our people were found. What a relief!

We were anxious about the others. Where is Dad? With the help of sympathetic French gendarmerie officers quartered here in Réalmont, my mother could hurry the official investigations. It was brain wracking, as Dad's address was either at home (!) or in the Army (!) where only his dog-tag number followed by "Somewhere in Belgium" could be mentioned.

Back home alone, Aunt Madeleine and cousin Colette

And we still didn't know for how long we would be here. A pleasant place if it was in favorable circumstances.

Réalmont was the capital of a Canton. Its colorful market attracted the whole area. Here too the odors were great: fruits, vegetables, flowers, herbs, and more. The choice of products produced elsewhere was getting reduced, and the dairywoman was stuck with the local cheeses. We didn't mind, they were very tasty, especially the Cantal presented in an enormous block she cut with a frightening long, sharp knife.

The market took place on the largest square, a pretty setting planted with plane trees (platanes). One side was occupied by the church, the three others by stylish houses used as stores of every kind. One of these sides "Les Couverts" (the covered), was a gallery that made the out-of-the-sun shopping pleasant and refreshing.

Danger – Gefahr – Danger

June 11, 1940—disaster! Mussolini declared war on Great Britain and on France. It would start at midnight. What was his strategy? Locals and refugees were troubled. The Club 27 met again. Was the truck still in good shape? Let's fill the tank before the events turn sour. Let's buy some provisions easy to travel with; supplies would be harder to find. Dad, where are we going to meet again?

The monthly big market opened as usual. Life kept going on anyway. It was maybe the last one. We would not miss the cattle market. We were fascinated by the huge oxen, the brown cows, the cute calves, lambs, piglets, chicks, ducklings. It was quite a show for the kids. The cattle merchants wore smocks and large black felt hats; they were discussing in their Occitan. We didn't understand a word, we were just amazed by the mimicry and the way they tapped in each other's hand when a deal was concluded. After that they would go to their nearest favorite café and, as they said, "Put a few pastis (fresh water and anise liquor) behind the tie."

Although with the worrying news, today, the atmosphere seemed less colorful.

Déroulement – Vorschrift – Unrolling

June 11 - Horrified, we heard that Paris had been bombed. Everybody was anxiously waiting for the U.S.A's answer to Prime Minister Paul Raynaud's S.O.S.

The Italian Army crossed the border at Menton. They didn't seem willing to do a full speed breakout past Nice, which had once been theirs. We hoped recapturing their historical former Nice would be enough!

On his wood-picking duties, my uncle met an old man who offered to teach him the art of fishing in the Dadou River. It would be a welcome supply to our daily bread. We received many messages from friends, nothing else.

June 14 - The Germans entered Paris. Deep sadness.

June 16 - The Russians invaded Lithuania. We felt lost. After school, the children didn't play anymore, they rushed home "in case of?" Fortunately, our neighbors kept coming every evening. We needed our mutual support.

June 17 - Marshal Pétain became prime minister; he contacted the Germans and asked their conditions for an eventual surrender. Hitler and Mussolini met the next day. The plenipotentiaries went back and forth again. Everybody was anxiously waiting for the end of this debacle.

June 22 - The armistice with the Germans was signed in Compiègne, and Hitler danced on the spot where the World War1 armistice had been signed.

June 24 - The cease-fire with the Italians was decided at 1 a.m. Even the sky was crying. The rain fell without a stop, quite exceptional in this region. Now France was cut in two. We were in the "safe part"—but for how long?

Visite – Besuch – Visit

The next day poor uncle came back from his first fishing lesson, disappointed, aware of his lack of skill and, worse, with his feet wet. However, he brought a few finny victims. They were absolutely delicious, and we encouraged him to give fishing another chance.

Many French and Belgian soldiers, who had previously received the South retreat order, could move again. The last days of June, a few of them arrived to meet their evacuated and re-found families. They had been regrouped in Béziers and Montauban, which was not far from Réalmont. For us, still no messages. Maman kept sending letters through every organization possible, but drew a blank. One morning we received a card from Uncle Maurice, Dad's brother, whose quarter was in Grisolles. He had got our address through Granville, and he announced his visit. A joyful event. My dear godfather arrived, tired and emaciated. He looked ten years older to me. From the family, he had the same news we had. He stayed rather silent about the drama he had gone through.

The next morning, as Uncle Marcel had located a dead, dry willow in a ditch, they both went about getting it out, cutting it in logs that they brought home. It wasn't easy. We were very thankful to Maurice, who, the same night, had to go back to his camp. The next morning the heavy rain came back and the temperature went down drastically. Due to that and to the general atmosphere, we all got sick. Sick

Uncle Maurice, our Réalmont visitor

enough to have high fever. The good doctor Aussenac came again and gave us some very effective medicine. As we could not name our disease, Michel, from the height of his almost four years, with a serious, eminent doctor's look, dropped, "It is a confusale disease" a brand new term which definitely stayed in the family's vocabulary. Maybe it's from there his future career was traced—he later became a country medical doctor.

Cérémonie – Feierlichkeit – Ceremony

July 4 - Maman's birthday. We didn't have the heart to celebrate it. The sun was back, Marcel went for a second, more fruitful, fishing party. In the afternoon, Maman took me by the hand and we went for a shopping tour. We stopped at the bakery, where we enjoyed the perfumed invasion of a batch of sourdough golden loaves coming out of the clay oven. We shared a huge éclair, a long, cream puff filled with custard and covered with sugar icing. The spirit of the day was not totally over shadowed.

July 14 - The French national Bastille Day. All the flags were half-mast. A Franco-Belgian procession went to the Veterans' monument and lay down bunches of flowers, which together formed the word PAX. What sort of peace could people expect?

A solemn mass was celebrated in the huge church, so different from the churches we knew. This one had two floors. The ground floor was occupied by the women and the children. The second, a gallery floor, was packed with men with their large, black felt hats on. Surprise! According to our tradition, to wear a hat in a church, for a man, was irreverent. We learned something every day.

Back home, the willow tree logs were waiting to be chopped.

Négocier – Verhandeln – Negotiate

The summer vacations started. Good-bye school! Where would we be in September?

We heard that some negotiations were going on about the Belgians' return. All the Belgian refugees were jumping around, except one little girl. Oh, Dad!

You'd better hurry up so we can stay here.

We saw another moving ceremony. A nurse who had been on the front line received a decoration for her exceptional acts of courage. Dominique's nephew, back from the Somme front and after he had escaped from a prisoners' convoy, had this optimistic comment: "We'll do better next time."

The first result of the negotiations: only the Flemish citizens could go home. It was the German's first tactic: "Divide and rule." So the people from Ghent we had met here left a few days later.

The sun and heat came back; we went to the forest. The berry season was over, so we picked wild cherries. They were so tart that they needed a large part of our ration of sugar to be edible.

July 21 - Belgian National Day. Many Belgian evacuees met at the local French Veterans' monument, where both French and Belgium anthems were respectfully played and sung.

Demain – Morgen – Tomorrow

The news came:

The Pierlot Belgian government evacuated in Bordeaux could not go back to Belgium anymore. A few of its members had already sneaked into England.

On the French side, the Lorrains and Alsatians could not go home either.

The Northern French citizens and the Belgian Walloons still had to wait.

People became very impatient. In spite of the official advice, some refugees tried to leave. The Club 27 decided to refurbish the truck. For the "Northward Ho!" it would be covered with a tarpaulin. Uncle Marcel dismantled his bike. As a souvenir, he drew a picture of our house that Michel called The Villa Minique. Meanwhile, my desperate Maman got the opportunity to get in touch with a smuggler, a "Passseur," who promised to deliver her letter into Dad's hands. The Passeurs found clandestine ways to take messages across regions and find people. She didn't mention how much the transaction had cost. The tricks AND treats era was open.

July 26 - The Club 27, and especially my aunt, could not stand to wait anymore. They didn't listen to reason, and we left. The good-bye to our local friends was difficult; each of us was in tears. I had the feeling Maman would have preferred to receive some news from Dad before leaving. Our future was so uncertain. Well, we'll see!

Essayer – Probieren – Try

We saw. Gone at 5 a.m., we were back at night. After being stopped in Montauban, we were blocked in Valence d'Agen, about one hundred miles away. Miraculously, we met the French captain who had helped us for our first trip. He convinced the group to wait one, or even better, two weeks longer. The Germans would not let any refugees cross the new border before being sure of control, security on the roads, gas, and food supplies. That made sense. Anyway, DECEPTION, except for you know who, that little girl for whom it was a personal blessing and new hope. Maybe, Dad would arrive from the anywhere he was before we could leave again.

Thank God, the villa was still untouched. We just had to get the key back from our surprised and generous Dominique. Our sympathetic grown-up friends shared grown-ups' feelings. Heads full of projects, the kids were happy!

Encore une fois – Noch einmal – Once more
The sessions on the bench re-started. We went back to the Dadou River, we enjoyed the shade under the dome of branches that the huge beech trees along the road were offering. We stocked up again on the perfume of thousands wild roses cascading down the high walls around the "Bagatelle," a property abandoned by its owner and close to our place.

In her grocery store, Miss Segur started to worry about the future serious restrictions. To manage her diminishing stock, she warned her customers, "I'll give you some, but not too much." One morning we found the bakery full of excitement. The wiry ladies looked like they were facing a tragedy. For the very first time a theft had been mentioned. People who could not walk a long distance every day used to put the money for the baker in their mailbox or in a tree hollow. That morning they had found neither the crusty bread nor the money. Oh! We were living in full decadence, no more sense of values, bla-bla, and all these freaky travelers going by, bla-bla- Whew, we were considered like respectable residents. Nice of them. Later on, we hit places where you were freaky for not being a city native. Honest ladies. One could not blame them. Life was sure changing, and not to its best.

Enfin – Endlich – At last
August 10 - Our friendly postman arrived on his

bike ringing like a madman and shouting: "A letter from the Red Cross." We rushed outside. At last it was from Dad! A letter? Well, a short message like a bubble of soap that Dad certainly had sent by the dozen through every organization still functioning. He had got Maman's letter from the passeur and had right away mailed an answer in every way possible. HE was home, **safe.** Our family and Uncle Marcel's were fine, but his brother was a prisoner of war, in good health anyway. Marcel's grandmother, in 1940, had been rescued by her nephew. A kind and knowledgeable French custom's agent had succeeded in calling the Belgian City Hall near where she lived to explain Marcel's departure. We were floating on cloud nine. Except my Aunt Irène, who was glad that our people were safe but had now other worries: what shape would her home and belongings be in, and more. She was very depressed and aggressive, blaming the longest stay here on "the others." Dear others, who were also waiting for a prompt departure. The next night, a new storm almost blew our roof away and the rain fell heavily.

Soulagement – Erleichterung – Relief

Thanks to the civil servants and teachers on board, who were now needed in Belgium, we received the green light for August 15. So we still had time for another cattle market before loading the truck, which was imaginatively equipped this time. The new wooden tarpaulin framework held hooks where we could attach little bags and cushions. We now had sort of a bench around the sides. No more sitting on our suitcases like on the first trip. Two passengers were added, a young Flemish couple who hadn't found any transportation. The husband knew a few words in French. Our unpracticed Flemish wasn't much better; we just kept smiling at each other. The good-bye was not as tragic as the first time. Aware of the difficulty of obtaining a travel authorization and my dear, safe father being blocked over there, I was eager to go back. I could wait and see for a while before planning our return to this beloved place. Well, you sometimes need to adopt a flexible attitude.

CHAPTER FIVE

The Way Back

Retour – Ruckreise – Journey back

The truck driver had received some instructions for the itinerary. Strangely enough, we were heading south again to Montpellier to join the refugees' caravan. In overcrowded Montpellier, we couldn't find any place to sleep. We kept going through the outskirts and further. Houses were sparse. We saw a man piling up the rest of the hay in his field. He showed us a place, at a distance, and said we could use it and went back to his work. All we found was a barn with a noisy and smelly horse in a corner. We quickly ate our leftover sandwiches before making our beds in the straw. Grandma's reduced mobility forced her to stay on the truck in her chair, which fortunately could be stretched out.

I don't know if you've ever met two dozen Belgians together. It's not melancholic. Funny comments were spreading from our hay "nests." With the fatigue and excitement, they soon became giggles and laughs. The curfew took a while to be established; the whinnying horse especially did not help. At dawn, we felt frozen, and to warm up, we ran to a close path. First we heard a strange noise, and then we saw the unexpected sea, the beautiful Mediterranean. Well, that sure marked the South limit to our expedition. We went back to the barn, put everything together, and stuck camp. We passed Montpellier again, got our complete itinerary, did some food shopping, and embarked "en route."

We had to reach the Rhône River at La Voulte by passing through the Cevennes mountain massif. It was not very high, around five thousand feet, but its roads were narrow and precipitous. In the multiple curves, the tarpaulin carcass creaked, and sometimes we had to hold it. Some passengers felt sick. The driver wouldn't stop. He had a schedule to follow or he just wanted to get out of the mess. So the nauseous had to make some openings in the tarpaulin and give their lunch and even breakfast back to nature. A hard ride.

At a nicely organized stop, Maman and I were welcomed in Pesmes. We were expected by a charming old couple who lived in a superb garden with peach trees in espalier all around. They offered us ripe, juicy, enormous, delicious fruits; we have never tasted the same since. They were avid to know about our odyssey. For them, they had been scared a few times, but, fortunately, without any personal damage.

Choc – Schlag – Shock

To me, it was the last relaxing intermezzo. Hardly gone from this last city in Ardèche, we hit the wide Rhône River. Our first real picture of war: an enormous, blown-up suspension bridge lay like a scrap pile in the middle of the river. I was petrified. Maman tried to distract me. She explained how now people would pass over a pontoon bridge, but it was as if a spring had broken in my mind. I had nightmares. From then on, our Club 27 plus the two young Flemish stayed rather silent; we realized that now, war was no longer a horror to see in newspapers and participate in at a distance, but a drama we would have to live through.

At present, we passed through empty villages; their inhabitants would come back later. We were heading to the Demarcation Line, the border between the French Free Zone and the German occupied zone. We passed Léchères, a city that, later on, lost many inhabitants poisoned by a bread, the wheat itself poisoned by rats. We stopped at the very welcoming butcher's place.

Everybody's apprehension grew as we approached the time to cross the Demarcation Line. Which attitude would the "Greens" (the Germans' uniform color) adopt toward us? How long would it take to go through the formalities? The adults, not full of happy memories about their rough bellicose visit twenty-six years ago, were mistrustful. The kids didn't know which way to turn.

Et voici – Und zwar – That's it

We finally reached the point on the direction of Pont-à-Mousson. I was curious to see what a German fighter looked like. I peeped through a tarpaulin hole and saw a soldier who, now, could be compare to the actor Gert Frobe in the James Bond movie *Goldfinger*, seated on his sidecar, red hair, red face, fat. He was laughing loudly while looking at our vehicle. I knew that, among our unusual equipment, a cooking pan hanging on the bike's wheel had been noticed before, but without such an effect. His reaction puzzled me. When I juxtaposed Hitler speaking and now him laughing, I wondered: were they always so noisy in their expressions? Even the swastika was flapping noisily in the wind.

Two tall, blue-eyed, blond officers came on board and meticulously checked our papers. Our truck was also inspected from top to bottom. They gave us our new assignment: next stop, Sedan. The control stop didn't take too long. Obviously they had received the order to make us believe they would be nice people to live with.

On our way, we passed through more empty villages, other partly skeletal villages, and some completely destroyed ones still smelling like cold smoke and spoiled non-harvest vegetation. Already a few intrepid young weeds were making their way through piles of crushed tiles and broken stones, pushing on what were former sidewalks. Part of a convoy, we couldn't slow down and the cracks in the tarpaulin didn't offer a large view. Nobody was talking.

Santé! – Prosit! – Cheers!

When we reached Sedan, we were guided to a former boarding school. The city was in a rather good shape but completely emptied of its twenty thousand inhabitants. Uneasy atmosphere. We just met a few groups of patrolling soldiers. We were taken in a huge, crowded refectory where some stew was served along with a piece of bread and a bowl of herb tea (dog-rose, in French: gratte-cul, scratch ass!) full of vitamins as they pointed out. Yuck! During the meal, the visit of a general was announced. He ceremoniously entered, stiff in his impeccable black SS uniform. He wore a monocle, which made his eye look rounder, accentuating his aquiline nose. He held a swagger stick. Sure of his commanding appearance, he walked along the central aisle. I swallowed another sip, thinking he should not be so proud if all he had to offer was this ugly mixture. An icy silence had fallen on the assembly. Absorbed in the effect of the unpleasant drink, I sarcastically deduced that no one liked that tea.

Perspective – Fernzeichnung – Prospect

The next morning our hearts trembled with joy. The driver could take the back roads he knew. We would be home soon. After lining up for gas—Maman was not in charge anymore—we left Sedan without any regret.

The countryside was more and more familiar. There was less wreckage. From time to time, we met pairs of German gendarmes on their big motorcycles. Then a serious question came to my mind. If still a gendarme, would Dad be forced to wear that verdigris uniform? I noticed the large badge they wore on their chest. It was a large, metallic piece, strangely decorated, like a commercial ad. What did "Gott mit uns" mean? I presumed it couldn't be "Bienvenue" (Welcome).

The Club 29's conversation picked up again. Tonight we would see our people. After these three adventurous months, would we all be different? Would the adults have the same jobs? Would the children still have the same schools and teachers?

At lunchtime, we found a restaurant lost in the middle of nowhere. The lady who had stayed home through the tumult still had some reserves. She could serve roast chicken and fresh tomatoes from her garden, a feast. We felt more relaxed, worries

pushed in the background to the point that my poor
aunt came out of her ivory tower asking for the recipe
of the especially tasty Dijon salad dressing.

The voyage was coming to its end. We reached the
Belgian border. The customs house was still there, so
were some of the custom's agents we knew and were
happy to see again. A few more formalities, quickly
done, and we were in Roisin. The Flemish couple
found a lift to the four-mile-away train station. They
weren't home yet.

Hearing an unusual motor, which could have been
the last truck in the area, people came out. Welcome,
handshakes, kisses, what excitement! Everyone
within earshot came soon to welcome us back from
our three month absence!

On our way home, the driver dropped every Club
27 ex-member at their door. We'll see you later. We
were the last ones, as we lived on the other edge of
the village. The driver put us, Yvette and her mother,
our luggage, and Grandma's chair on our sidewalk.
He coldly gave Maman the bill for his driving and left.
Why such a hurry? He could give it to my father the
next day. Anyway, this bill, like any kind of money
business, was on hold. The banking system was not
releasing funds and we were adjusting to German
Marks. For now, what each of us could count on for
sure were his own blessings: being back home, safe
and healthy. For the driver, he also had kept his
truck and helped his seventeen private passengers on
top of the ten official ones of us. Back in his village,
he sure didn't want to be considered as a friendly
"official" helper; it could complicate his life among the
local population.

Chez nous – Zuhause – At home

As he didn't expect us so soon, Dad was not at home when we arrived. A predictable but minimal mess was still visible in garden and park, nothing frightful. More raking and planting lay ahead. We walked around the house, which seemed in good shape. I climbed on a suitcase to look through a kitchen window. In the sun, the light-colored furniture, the electric stove, and the large coal furnace, gave the impression of a deluxe place compared to the poor content of our Villa Dominique.

Meanwhile Dad arrived. We had anxiously waited for that precious moment, and for so long, we remained speechless. There was too much to be said. We fell in each other's arms with so much joy and gratitude to our protectors. You remember St. Benoît? Yes, we really had been protected.

Dad let us in. At first view, things looked familiar and the lingering smell of a fresh cleaning was welcome. Apparently some supplies had been reserved for this long-awaited celebration. Dad brought himself plates and glasses; they were unmatched. In the heat of the conversation, no one seemed to care, as I had kept in mind, Dad was not a "house-person." Anyway, he could prepare some robust military dishes with lentils, herbs, and bacon. From that dinner, I remember the mock leek-soup quickly made out of what was available in the neglected garden and could taste like some leek. A famous leek soup was a souvenir that brought a touching smile around the tablecloth-less table. Years before, Maman had such a flu that she had to stay in bed. Terribly thirsty, she was convinced that only a leek soup could help her. Well intended, Dad had decided to fix it at once. In hurry, he hadn't paid enough attention to the tricky leeks. They viciously kept some deeply hidden—sand. The soup required a serious straining before Maman could appreciate it. Still amused, she said, "I needed that soup so much and I was so thankful, that I would have eaten it with a fork."

During the meal, we exchanged some news we hadn't gotten through the short messages. After dinner and after a longer hug, I was so exhausted that I went to bed, my own, still there, little bed. Paying no attention to the unmatched but clean, wrinkled sheets, I slept like a log, a happy, heavy log.

A doctor friend, a category of people who could have a car, came the next day to fetch Grandma, happily rid of her chair, and bring her back to Havré where Grandpa was anxiously waiting. On the way, he dropped off my uncle, my recovering aunt and little Michel. In Genly, they found their house in the same state Dad had found ours, with almost empty cabinets.

That first evening Dad had been very discreet about the war developments. Too involved in it, he would talk later. As for the house, we noticed the walls had been cleaned up but still had strange stains. Dad told us then that he had come back to find it in total chaos. Our house had been visited by refugees and locals who had helped themselves, followed right after by soldiers who had finished emptying the wine cellar, left the broken empty bottles all around, and destroyed whatever had come into their crazy minds. They had thrown jars of marmalade on the crucifix, on the floors and even in Maman's sewing kit, gluing together threads, silk hankies, and buttons. In the garden, they also had practiced shooting with a large part of the china tableset. Only one visitor had acted civilly, a German captain who had written a note to apologize for taking one of Dad's white shirts and leaving a dirty one. Dad understood German— souvenir of the Occupation in Germany after WWI— and he appreciated the gesture in spite of the shirt being three sizes too large.

Détail – Einzelheit – Detail

We started to search places where we could still find linen, sheets, towels, kitchen appliances, and more. We were as impoverished as in the villa. My far-sighted mother, a knitting fan, cleaned out the most remote country stores' wool scraps. The colors didn't always match, but so what? Later on she would work that out. I remember an atrocious green mixed with white, like a cross stitch, that became my favorite pullover for the years to come.

The inhabitants came back in waves. Everyone had gone through frightening, even perilous, adventures. Unfortunately, the sad list of missing citizens was extending every day. One of our young neighbors, René, had been killed on the front line. Most of the civilian victims had been lost in France, in the severe bombing in Cambrai, a few hours after we had passed through. My mind began to understand and accept the "after loss" stage. I personally knew some victims, not only among my school partners, but now also among many grown-ups. Everybody was specially touched by a young widower whose wife had been killed in the bombing. It was unusual at that time for a father to take such motherly care of his very young boy.

Eclat d'obus – Schrapnell – Shrapnel

Dad started to talk. On May 16, his friend and he arrived in Tournai on their bikes and immediately got caught in a heavy bombing. Trees and debris fell all over. They lay in a ditch on an avenue. When Dad pushed his friend's foot to know how he was doing, he had no answer. He crawled closer and saw his neck had been entirely opened by a bomb shrapnel. The first shock.

Après – Nachher – After

As for my father's job, nothing had changed yet. He still reported to his former superiors. The Germans took the reins smoothly.

The last Belgian government evacuated to Bordeaux had been transferred to Vichy, in the French Free Zone. Two of its members had already escaped and had flown to England. As our villa Dominique had no radio, we had missed the French General de Gaulle's June 18 appeal sent from a kitchen of the British Broadcasting Corporation, known as the BBC, in London. It was the first message of a man determined to act and devote his life to rallying the patriots and bringing back to life the prolific roots of their country. So some hope was already in the air.

The railways were repaired mile after mile. We could go and see how Grandpa had done through this period. He was so happy to count us all together and also rejoiced that Grandma felt so good. He was himself in good health and spirits, fascinated by our stories. On his side, he had stayed home, filled the food bins, closed shutters and doors, and been lucky enough not to be disturbed. Dear optimist

Sample of Grandfather's work

Grandpa was now waiting for his wood carvers return. Grandpa's ébénisterie workshop was far from being full; he had only kept one sculptor and one assistant. Their cabinet work consisted of repairs of antique furniture damaged by bombs or vandals or copies when the repair was impossible. "Let's start the work again, many injured treasures are in need of being repaired," he said. Because the German Army had passed on the other side of the forest, Havré had stayed out of the heavy battles. Aunt Germaine hadn't seen a German soldier on her chimney.

Jouer – Spielen – Play

Luckily all my friends were back. How eager were we to narrate our mutual experiences, sometimes with a little fantasy. We didn't go back to our former games like Hide and Seek, Indians and Cowboys,

Cops and Robbers. We had grown up too fast, like years instead of months. Bicycle races would still have been attractive if our bikes hadn't been stolen with no possibility of replacement.

In our state of mind, we created a private headquarters to discuss events. Our meetings turned out to be occasions to exchange news and opinions. We thought our war was finished. Of course, the British Empire was still at war. Then we remembered times where English soldiers had been rude to us when we had crossed their paths. Once our driver had been rebuffed with a sharp "Shut up!" (those became my first English vocabulary words) when he had asked for some water for the truck. One boy's father, an allied soldier who had participated to the last battle in Dunkerque, had been thrown overboard from an escaping British boat, a ship considered "British only." The British hasty withdrawal from France was chaotic. The British had already forgotten the help their Navy had and was still receiving from French and Belgian boats. The British had confiscated the French boats in the English harbors, so that, we generously admitted, the Germans couldn't steal them. But couldn't they have been better organized and not killed 1297 sailors when they had destroyed part of the French Navy in Mers-El-Kebir in Algeria last July? So, following our children's cruel and prompt judgment, we thought that the bombings of London and its surroundings would just teach them a lesson. Talking about lessons, Winston Churchill had the Royal Air Force bomb Berlin for revenge.

The next important matter for us: the schools would reopen soon.

CHAPTER SIX

Secrecy

Loi – Recht – Law

The German occupier, who only had about twelve hundred military men to control the eleven million Belgian and northern French citizens' administrations, started to spin his web. He jammed the British Broadcasting Corporation, censored the mail, and more. Anyone caught listening to the BBC was severely punished. From there forward, listening required a prudent secrecy.

The trickiest ways were found to catch the verboten BBC. Correspondents created codes to communicate. It could be fun. The satirical singers still performed, sometimes applauded by some German soldiers on leave, who didn't get the message, which was "lost in translation." Singers could ridicule Germany in front of German soldiers who did not understand the language completely.

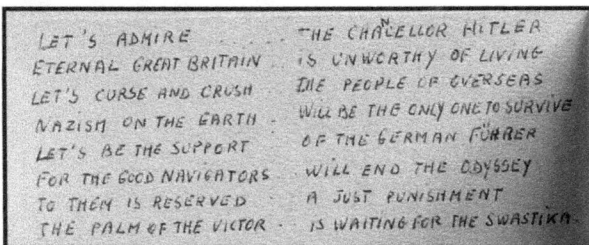

LET'S ADMIRE	THE CHANCELLOR HITLER
ETERNAL GREAT BRITAIN	IS UNWORTHY OF LIVING
LET'S CURSE AND CRUSH	THE PEOPLE OF OVERSEAS
NAZISM ON THE EARTH	WILL BE THE ONLY ONE TO SURVIVE
LET'S BE THE SUPPORT	OF THE GERMAN FÜHRER
FOR THE GOOD NAVIGATORS	WILL END THE ODYSSEY
TO THEM IS RESERVED	A JUST PUNISHMENT
THE PALM OF THE VICTOR	IS WAITING FOR THE SWASTIKA

Audacious double meaning pamphlet

A new pro-German officer named Van Coppenole was assigned to supervise the direction of the gendarmerie. After reading the Van Coppenole's list of new wartime crimes to his men, my father's comment was, "Our duty is to run after their outlaws, but to catch some of them is another story." His line was drawn. A line understood and responsibly accepted by his team.

Confronter – Konfrontieren – Confront

Our world was in the rebuilding process. Our dear cousins, the Noëls, were back in Quiévrain. They invited us to celebrate the occasion. Our thoughtful cousin Simone had felt it would be better for me, before school started, not to be alone to see the places where many friends had been lost. Even so, for a while, I shivered when passing in front of the destroyed homes I knew.

Life went on for us busy children. When September came, we were happy to go back to school. As so much time had been lost, the Academy suggested we start classes all over. We lost a school year. I didn't mind, as I was a year ahead.

We had the same teachers, only the program was a bit different. There was a red label glued on the book covers with the note: "Revised according to the directions of the Classical Works Control Commission." The comments on historical facts were slightly different from the ones we had learned before. Among the other courses, we still had French and Flemish; English had disappeared. German was on the new list except for the pupils who took Latin and Greek. Good! I could escape that despotic croaking.

Now we had one free afternoon a week, on Thursday,

instead of the three we had before, which were then reserved for movies, theater, concerts, and excursions. At lunchtime, we received a bowl of soup and a glass of light beer (we were in Belgium). Sandwiches were a challenge for our mothers. Rationing was on, with a small amount per ticket. Cheese and sausage sliced so thin you could see the future through it. No more chocolate, bananas, oranges, lemons, and more, just the local fruit production, diminished by a large portion reserved to the Third Reich.

Because of the lack of diesel fuel, the rail car, the Micheline, had been replaced by a wood-fed streetcar we guessed came out of a museum. The monster ran only twice a day. I had to leave at 6 a.m. and come back at 6 p.m.

The classes started with the excitement of the reunion and the new subjects in the program.

Imagine the confusion created by the original way the Greeks wrote their letters and the Germans their Gothic alphabet. We didn't totally escape the German classes. The history teacher had the most fascinating way of dragging us out of the present situation; ancient Egypt would surely be able to keep us alert. Well, the sun could still be shining.

Campagne – Kampagne – Campaign

One of Dad's friends came for a visit. He brought Maman a priceless present: two pounds of flour cleverly hidden in an official roll of papers (the food inspectors were abundantly cruising around). When he saw Dad, he rushed to him shouting a strange "Schnouf. Schnouf"; so did my welcoming father. Maman was laughing, I was puzzled. It was their

"Chasseurs Ardennais" sign of recognition. It sounded like the grunting of the wild boar embroidered on their badge. In front of a cup of malt slightly perfumed with chicory, they shared their war experiences.

They had been together on the front line. It had sometimes been funny. For example, on the last, mixed-up days, when, due to the suddenly changed orders, the confused operator had sent them to a mispronounced place; they ended up on an isolated farm. After the camouflage of their bikes, they had carefully approached, guns drawn, almost giving a heart attack to an old couple who had refused to leave their home. It was about lunchtime. Of course, no army kitchen was in sight, so the farmers had insist on serving them a heap of boiled potatoes swimming in a tasty bacon gravy. A feast in these circumstances.

We also learned the reason why Dad's helmet had such a dent on the top. While cleaning a post full of Germans, one had arrived from the back. Not to alarm other fighters with a noisy shot, the soldier attacked Dad with his gun butt. The German "was" a big guy they said. Not wanting to give any gory details in front of me, meaning of WAS left to interpretation, but I do not think the big guy survived.

What we didn't know yet was that Dad had been buried alive under the ground, blown away by a canon shell. Two Chasseurs Ardennais had come to the rescue. Only Dad's head and one arm were entirely out of the heavy sand when both of them were killed by machine gun fire. Then I understood why I could sometimes catch my father looking far, far away with so much sadness in the eyes.

That was THE story to tell to my H.Q. partners.

They were impressed, and without a dissenting voice, we decided to put these two unknown heroes in our "Honor Box," an imaginative box in which we treasured, like litanies, the names of people or events touching our patriotic souls.

Avion – Flugzeug – Plane

A sort of routine went on, disturbed by the Japanese invasion in Indochina. A new obsessive problem. The Americans, the Dutch, and the British had organized a helpful blockade to limit the Japanese expansion in Asia. For our young H.Q., the Indochinese were people who wore large straw hats and ate rice. To be attacked made them closer to us. We followed the news.

The British helping them regained our sympathy, increased by the fact that now we could hear their planes flying over, on their way to attack Germany. We recognized their motors. They were going . . . Vrouuuuuuuuu . . . instead of the Messerschmitts' Wha . . . wha . . . wha . . . These sounds were heavier when the planes were loaded with bombs.

Enfant – Kind – Child

Winter was here. The hours had been changed to follow the German system. No outside light permitted, with the benefit that stars and constellations could be seen much better. The Grande Ourse, Ursa Major, or Big Dipper, whatever its name is, shined in front of my bedroom window. With a finger, I could trace a line between the carriage limits, follow with a large curve for the horses, and end up on the capricious twinkling coachman, the smaller star on the last but one. I considered it a reassuring reliable old friend.

Poetry aside, 6 a.m. was drowned in an unpractical pitch black. With the minimum of heat in the houses and at school, we went out dressed like Eskimos, and we didn't take too much off inside.

The old housekeeper opened the doors at our arrival before 7 a.m. The central heating was off, so he started the fires in old cast-iron stoves. It took a serious dose of acrid smoke and a long time to warm up. With that and the unique lamp hanging from the high ceiling, the atmosphere wasn't too great. The ten o'clock cup of "liquid" was welcomed. Fortunately, the kitchen here hadn't picked the Sedan-dog-rose-tea's recipe.

Every Monday we received a weekly dose of vitamins and some cod liver oil capsules. As the vitamins tasted like lemon candies, our provision was gone by the end of the day. No one could stand the cod liver oil. We always succeeded in planting it at the foot of a young tree. We were convinced that it was the reason why that tree was growing so nicely. Kids!

The temperature went down to minus twenty degrees C (minus four F). We had some snow and thick ice. Once, on our yard, like on a mirror, a black bird, alone in a pink and orange large patch of sunset, looked like an exclamation mark. I wished I could have painted it.

Even our archaic tramway had to be heated with a cast-iron stove. Because many men were away, now prisoners of war, plants and orchards were laid aside, and many gardens and fields remained unproductive. Not too much could be put on the tables. Our daily rations consisted of only 11.7 grammes of butter, 30 gr. of margarine, our only daily fat ingredients for flavoring and cooking. In comparison: 28 gr. = one ounce. Our other daily rations were 35 gr. of meat and 250 gr. of bread or starch, such as potatoes. The black market was already flourishing.

Faim – Hunger – Hunger

Watched by the German authorities and locals "pros," who supported them, we had to set the example. Obey the law, starve, or be wise, which we did. My parents knew many farmers from whom we had bought products before the war. Some agreed to provide a little supplement, a very little as they didn't dare to charge the price they asked the city dwellers. These prices had gone five to ten and more times higher. With this reduced amount, to complete a minimum stock, we needed to buy an annual thirty kilos of wheat and a monthly two hundred fifty grams of butter. For that, Dad had to visit sixteen farms. Maman and I walked a solid hour every Saturday to bring back two supplementary pints of milk so skimmed it was blue. Sometimes we had the luck to find one egg, even two in the propitious season.

The government organized the "Winter Help" to assist those people in extreme need. They tried to provide clothing and even opened soup kitchens. Compared to some other citizens, we were still privileged.

The sixth of December was the children's feast in Belgium. Saint Nicolas brought toys and goodies. During the last session of our H.Q., we convinced ourselves that we were too old for childishness;

imagination would be more productive to refill and embellish our souvenirs. Anyway the ersatz (substitute) candies tasted yucky. Our creative mothers filled the gap with some cookies, following recipes created to use what was available.

Lettre – Brief – Letter

We could mail censored letters to the whole family. Although we were in the Greater Reich, borders still existed and were not easy to cross. We missed our family members who lived in France.

Aunt Victoria, her daughter Marguerite, and her sister Boka had left Granville and were back to Douai in the North. Marguerite was teaching again at the École Normale. My paternal grandparents and Uncle Charles had returned to Revin in the Ardennes. Everyone was fine. Grandma had sent us the hundred recipes to prepare tuna fish she had from their host the fisherman, but we had no more fish. Sea fishing was verboten, to stop any connection with the U.K. and other enemies.

Aunt Madeleine was back home with her little daughter Colette only. Her mother and her two sweet aunts had died in Nevers. Fortunately, Uncle Maurice was back home too; he had escaped from a prisoner camp.

Dad then talked about his own two escapes. His stratagem? He had pretended to help direct a prisoners' column and . . . whiz! The first time on his bike, he had been easily recaptured by a German motorcyclist. The second time, he waited to be alongside a forest that he could go into quickly with his bike to hide, and bye-bye.

At that time, the situation was so confused that nobody had seemed overly surprised either to see him wandering alone in a military uniform or coming back home by himself.

Noël – Weihnachten – Christmas

Just the three of us celebrated Christmas. No more midnight mass. Because of the curfew, the streets had to be empty at 9 p.m. Maman and I sang carols, Dad's voice couldn't match with any tune. We rebuild our traditional crib with the few left pieces we had found. Maman had been very busy knitting for the three of us. For me she had made a scarf, a bonnet, and a pair of gloves to match my pullover. Was I proud! That evening even the dinner was fancier due to Maman's planning. It seemed we ate a feast of our entire monthly ration of meat that meal. Instead of buying the sticky black bread, Maman had bought the flour and sieved it. Mixed with some illegal white floor and mashed potatoes, the result was pretty good. With the bran she had made a sort of gingerbread. How did she replace the disappeared exotic spices? She even had shaped it like the traditional bûche (log) garnished with a touch of powdered sugar to replace the traditional pink sugar Baby. It was our first wartime Christmas.

Haine – Hass – Hate

In June, Hitler dreamed of saving the world from the communist system. To give a crusade appearance, he put the name Operation Barbarossa on his bloody attack against Russia. His army turned in the direction of Leningrad and Moscow.

Léon Degrelle, a politician who had formerly been known as an anti-communist and the founder of the "Rex" party, wanted to attract the occupant's attention by assuring the German Army of his sympathy and collaboration.

In Belgium, to prove his good will, Léon Degrelle created the Walloon Legion to help on the front line. He found four thousand adherents. The two Flemish movements, the V.N.V. and the De Flag, found ten thousand. These groups also had members in the territorial Gestapo. In fact, if his maneuver gave him the pros' support, but he lost quite a lot of his previous supporters.

People were dumbfounded, chiefly in our village, that one of residents became a Black Legion big wheel. Another one was a "Daddy's boy goody two shoes" became a Black Legion big wheel. However, we were glad the Russians would no longer be Hitler's allies. The end of the German-Russian non-aggression pact created new demand for Belgium Rexist forces.

Volontaire – Freiwillig – Voluntary

After the Black Legion was formed, my father was discreetly contacted by scouts who had started to organize what would quickly become the diversified Resistance. The next week he received a strange visit. A "Gott mit uns," a German gendarme, arrived on his motorcycle. He didn't stop his motor, he just said, "Be careful, some people are sending denouncement letters to the Kommandantur" (German police's office), and he took off. Honest and fair—colleague?

German propaganda tried to convince people that denunciation was a respectable form of patriotism.

That reporting a neighbor's questionable behavior to authorities was proper. Our standards were different. The first "Resistants" acted in the Postal Service, when filching denouncement letters. They saved many lives but fatally lost a lot of theirs.

The Red Cross forwarded packages to the P.O.Ws. Every lady was knitting scarves and socks. They had saved their tickets to bake cookies and obtain material and canned goods. Some of them became the "war Godmother" of a specific P.O.W. Kids sent their best drawings and inspired poems to cheer up P.O.Ws.

Haute Société – High Society – High Society

An unexpected explosive news unsettled the Belgian world. During Sunday Mass, the priest read a letter from the Bishop Van Roey to announce that King Léopold III had married Ms. Liliane Baels.

What? A POW married, at home?! The people were more royalist than the king and objected not only because of the mistiming, but that SHE was a commoner. Even more, she came from a family considered to be "pro," indignity nobody could loudly mention at the time. The anti-royalists played on the ordinary people's heartstrings to remind them that he was the widower of the nation's beloved and venerated queen Astrid, princess of Sweden, their three young children' s mother. The Queen had been killed in a car accident in Kussnacht (Switzerland) at the age of thirty. According to an uncontrolled and tendentious press, Liliane, an arrogant beauty, even if she had received the title of Princess de Rethy, had only been alleged to be the children's governess' supervisor. Moreover, she was the daughter of the actual Occidental Flander Governor. The foreign royal families and the aristocracy blackballed the new couple. The royal future was dark, the worm was in the apple.

At the beginning of the war, some marriages had legally been made possible, inevitably at a distance. Some couples, whose wedding had been interrupted by the army's general mobilization, had the possibility to have an oath friend or parent sign the civil document. A groom-less ceremony. Our school director's daughter had that privilege. From that peculiar wedding, I still remember Valerie coming back home with her shiny eyes full of a mixture of dreamy joy, pride, and sadness.

With all these events swirling around, personal issues stayed in the background.

Birthdays were sparsely celebrated. We just sent cards; homemade practical presents were reserved to a limited circle. Fortunately, we could go and visit the family members who didn't live too far away— not so easy, however, as the restricted, overcrowded, often delayed civilian trains forced us to travel in poor conditions. Later on, with the allied bombing, train travel became hazardous and perilous.

Lapin – Kaninchen – Rabbit

In July, children welcomed the summer vacations. They could recuperate from the rough, long school days' requirements. The weather was great and the sun was setting down around 11 p.m. To us, it looked like endless time we filled with unusual occupations: help with the problematic shopping, pick fruits and vegetables eagerly planted in spring, cut feeding grass for the rabbits. They ate as much as a cow, these rabbits. Huge white animals with red, shiny eyes, they were the only meat supplement we could raise. We had no cereal grains to feed hens, and if we did, we would have to declare the egg production and give a part away. Some lucky people who had a smell-and-sound-proof hidden place could raise a well-treated pig commonly named "Adolph."

We took long walks in the forest; we climbed the "Caillou-qui-bique" (the stone that sticks out). We explored the unique cave and swam in the Honelle River. We took advantage of living in a nice countryside still out of the uproar.

Traditional vacations were out. Very few places could accommodate guests and were much too expensive. The preferred Belgian spot, the seacoast, was verboten (forbidden), as Hitler had decided to build the Atlantic Wall. He planned extensive coastal defenses to keep out Allied invaders away. The Todt Organization would do the work.

The official radio only gave victorious German news: Leningrad was suffering, many Allied boats had been destroyed by numerous German submarines, the Allies' planes had been knocked out by the dozens, and more. With the maximum of precaution, and attention, we could capture the BBC. There the news was a little different: German centers of communication and transportation had been bombed, the spreading out of the Allies' help was effective and more.

Our H.Q. found a shelter in the common laundry room. At the time, the use of electricity was limited; the wash-machines could still wash but not heat the water.

A huge wood stove had been installed; that's why the place was comfortable. We enhanced our equipment with a huge world map and plenty of homemade different pin flags to stick on the battlefields. It sure taught us more geography than the school program. We created a camouflage in case of an unexpected visit by some pro German. We used a burlap potato bag to hide our map. We had plenty to do.

Bataille – Schlacht – Battle

Right now the Russian battles were the center of attention. We traced the front according to the news. One pin on Leningrad, one pin on Moscow, and another one on Helsinki, as Finland was now friendly with Germany.

After a serious discussion, our H.Q. decided to forget the conflicts started before we had been directly concerned. Since we were born, the adults' conversations had always contained worries due to wars and political problems. Too young to participate, we nevertheless had kept in mind a long list of repeated names.

We remembered:

The awkward situation in Rheineland with Germany reoccupying that territory.

In 1934: the assassination of Dolfuss, the Austrian Chancellor.

In 1936: the Popular Front, Left Hand victory in France with Léon Blum at its head.

Guernica, the massacre of civilians in Spain during their civil war.

In 1938: Haile Selassie was attacked by the Italians. I knew he had been proclaimed Negus in Ethiopia the year I was born, and Dad had escorted him when he had officially visited a coal mine in Belgium. In Munich, a treaty was signed to end the German-Czech problem, a conflict pushing the "Sudetes"-Germans out and progressively replacing them with a German occupation.

The Anschluss, the imposed German union of Austria with Germany.

In 1939: Poland was surprisingly attacked by the Germans, helped by the Russians.

The Mannerheim line in Finland, also attacked by the Germans.

We kept hearing about Chiang Kai-shek who was an active anti-communist in China, also Nehru and Ghandi in India.

Roosevelt was our Idol.

Churchill, Chamberlain, Eden were members of the British government.

Pierlot was the First Minister in Belgium.

Daladier was the French First Minister when they went at war with Germany in 1939 and so, and so.

Coming back to our selected map, we put a pin on our year 1940's war predecessors:

Denmark, Norway off their coast in April the, Narvick naval German-English-French battles.

Then in May invasions Holland, Luxembourg, Belgium, and part of France.

In June, the Russian invasion in Lithuania.

We also had to look at Asia: one pin on Indochina.

Then in Africa: one pin on Egypt where the Italians had tried to beat the English, one pin on Tripoli where Mussolini was pushed back, chased by the Desert Rats; even Rommel had to come to his rescue. We knew Rommel, the general who had taken Cambrai and Rouen, forcing us to speed up in 1940. Hitler had recently named him commander for the Atlantic Wall operation. The Wall would be built from Denmark to South France. Hitler hadn't followed his project to invade England, and he was sure afraid to see the Allies coming out from there.

CHAPTER SEVEN

Danger

Clandestinité – Klandestinität – Underground

From then, my father started his parallel activities. The first meeting took place in a quiet, discreet place, an isolated cemetery with, as participants: one Russian, two French, and him. They would be a basic link of a long chain that would repatriate, to England via France and Spain, the downed allied pilots saved by another link, or "necessary persons." Exciting, isn't it? To act clandestinely pushed us into a deeper isolation.

"Don't say any word that could attract certain people's attention," he said. "Don't bring anybody home where we could have illegal material or a guest."

We also would attentively listen to and interpret some code messages from the BBC. At that time, I realized my inclusion in the process. From still-privileged and protected child I had passed to active, protective partner.

Fortunately, life is stronger than the events; the children kept growing and they made their own adjustments. School was the best antidote. There we could act like teenagers. We sure did. Did we have fun and giggles! On our way home with our friends, we whispered anti-German jokes—it let us feel like conspirators.

The German Army was progressing to Moscow and Kiev, besieging Leningrad, and triumphantly making a lot of victims.

Attaque – Angriff – Attack

Unforgettable December 7. Without any war declaration, Japan attacked the U.S. bases in Pearl Harbor and in the Philippines. Then Japan attacked the British in Hong Kong, in Malaya, in Borneo, and the Dutch in Indonesia. Ghastly! We found the process revolting and worrying. If the Americans were "in the bath" like us, would they stop to think about Europe?

A second winter was there, and the situation was even worse. The year 1942 promised to be hard. Three or four times a week, Dad spent part of the night crossing the border with pilots. Maman was more and more nervous. Sometimes when Dad was too late, she couldn't help to come in my room. We would pray and sweat together.

To hold Dad's camouflage, Maman, with whatever was still on hand, made him different outfits to match the seasons' colors, even the moonlight. Of good Ardennaise origin, Dad could notice the minor change made in the discreet marks he had traced in daytime. He could tell if someone else had used his path, his awareness and stealth skills were paramount for his safety. His safety and success of his missions depended on his stealth and awareness.

Only once did things almost turn bad. He and his guests had escaped from a German mobile patrol. Dad came home ignoring that he had a bullet wedged between his bike rim and the tire. When he stopped in the bike shelter, the tire exploded. Dad ran home, promptly dashed in the house while removing his unusual attire. He then opened the bedroom window in his undershirt and joined the neighbor's anxious questions' chorus. Soon after, he came down, pistol in hand. Of course, all his men had done the same. He did his best to keep them away from his bike. After he had found and picked out the bullet, he called them: "Never mind, it just came from a tire." At that time, the quality of the tires was so poor that it made sense to say the change of temperature had made it explode. Whew! Our heartbeat calmed down, and we nervously laughed at the adventure. It took a while before we fell asleep. We thought someone had tried to kill him.

Astuce – Schlauheit – Astuteness

A few days later, some friends called Dad to introduce a couple and their teenage boy who had planned to spend a period of convalescence in a certain hotel isolated at the edge of the forest. The guests were obviously Jewish and worried. As every new resident in the territory had to register, Dad talked to the doctor, and together they made plans about eventual questions and agreed to ignore, for now, the convalescent's presence. To declare someone sick, even hidden under a common Christian name, was dangerous in case of the Gestapo checking seriously. Germans would check closer; they were not tender with abnormal persons. We knew a German family who had to hide their Down syndrome son. Germans eradicated people with that condition in their own country.

Motif – Ursache – Motive

The Jews were going through a very difficult time. The Germans had worked on the plot a long time ago; they accused Jews of every possible crime, making them detested. Then had come the pretext to relocate the ethnic groups, as Germany wanted to protect the "Gut Aryan" race, an expression that had easily turned into a joke as, when translated in French, "Bon Aryen" pronounced like "Bon à rien" meant "Good to nothing."

For the Jews, the heavy control had started. They had to register in the Kommandantur to receive a large yellow star, a badge they constantly had to wear in order to be immediately identified. People who disobeyed were arrested. The others would be sent to a region, sort of a reservation, where they would live together according to their beliefs. That was what the Germans wanted us to believe. We never heard about atrocities and extermination. The secret about the concentration camps stayed well covered.

The Belgian gendarmerie never received the order to cooperate in the action. Germans didn't trust them enough? Anyway, more Jews became suspicious; they found shelters mostly in families, presbyteries, and convents.

As often as possible, the kids of owner of the nearby Crèmerie and I went to play with the poor, isolated boy. Materially he didn't seem to lack anything. His parents obviously could afford it, but he was lost here at the edge of the forest. We could wander inside of the property but not play too close to the next property, where "you never know." We brought some old books. My favorites were the Jules Verne adventures, the

Hergé's Tintin, I didn't dare to add the Comtesse de Ségur's stories that I found too girlish for him.

No TV at the time. The radio was not too interesting: sweetened news; ditties we knew by heart, sung by Maurice Chevalier, Tino Rossi, Rina Ketty, Annabella, and more. From the German side: Sarah Leander with her deep, masculine voice, Isle Werner who whistled like a bird, Liselotte Pulver (we named her Liselotte Pullover), and Cy, but nothing from over the channel. Marlene Dietrich with her "Lily Marlene" and Josephine Baker with her "Mon Pays et Paris" were active in the opposite camp.

The only movie theater was in Quiévrain. To match the transportation and the curfew wasn't simple. Anyway, beside the news, which praised the courageous and victorious German warriors, the films were only musicals, the heroes were tap dancers. Marika Rök (Marie Carrot for us) acted in every film. So we didn't go too often.

The "Winter Help" organized some local theater plays to raise funds for the benefit of POWs still held in Germany. At one of the village's schools, old Sister Pharaïlde even presented the seventh grade girls to recite together a serious fable of La Fontaine, "La Carpe et les Carpillons" ("The carp and the young carps") Using ridiculous gestures for their age and size, they had been praised by their families only. It was so funny that it stayed in our family's vocabulary. Just mentioning the title still replaces a comment about anything gauche.

Of course, the forest boy, who could not be seen in our dangerous village, never attended these joyful parties. He could just listen to our ironic report.

Bravade – Trotz – Bravado

One morning the Kommandantur sent three "specialists" to retrace the border between France and Belgium. Because of his legal job, my father had to show them around. The subject was awkward as, because of a particularity of our region, there were a few straddling houses, part in France – part in Beligium. Of course, the visitors wanted to judge on the spot. As they had a car, "innocently" Dad took them to Lodie's place. Lodie was a character UNIQUE.

She ran a store in Belgium, and her kitchen was in France. Because of the dirt road it was built on, you could imagine that, before the war, Lodie had not made a fortune with customers of passage. She had been a master smuggler. At that time, tobacco and alcohol were passed through the border by expert teams, on foot and with specially trained dogs. When she had faced brutal competition, she had secretly solved the problem by herself. Lodie was aware of everything, but we were never quite sure of her methods — only that she always got her way. She was always a precious source of information. She appreciated what Dad did, and she was on his side.

She immediately understood Dad's tactics and made the Germans' visit as unpleasant as possible. Painting the picture, let's say that Lodie, in her old days, had become "untidy." Her clothes and her person had not touched deep water for quite a while. Her kitchen was a mess. As a friendly gesture, she pushed a few hens down the table, wiped it with the corner of her apron, and offered a cup of pseudo coffee in clean cups shined with the other corner of her apron. Dad accepted her offer, which embarrassed the three others and pushed them to do the same.

No one could sit, as the chairs were covered with used towels, newspapers, cats, and more. The surveyors obviously wanted to shorten the visit, but Dad was giving as many details as possible about a doorstep, which could be in France or in Belgium. Lodie was graciously adding more information. The guys' faces were turning as green as their uniforms. To go out, they had to cross through her filthy store that still sold a few garden tools and mousetraps. Suddenly, mundane, Lodie exclaimed: "Excuse me, I have been waiting for too long, I must go."

Then she took the deep tray of the scale and, standing up, urinated in it. You could say it was the last straw. The three visitors took off. Dad was suffocating with interior giggles, and Lodie had the most devilish winner's look in her piercing eyes.

The specialists silently brought Dad home. They left and never came back. If they were also interested in racial particularities, we guessed it took a very long time before they found out which group Lodie belonged to.

A few days later, two boys in our neighborhood were arrested and driven to the Kommandantur in Mons, deeply worrying their family. They were liberated in the evening after their dark hair, eyes, and their profile had been recognized as issued from a Spanish grandma and not from a you-know-who. At the same time, Gypsies, whom we also call Bohemians or Romanichels, were equally considered as a stain on the Aryan shield.

Bouger – Bewegen – Move

After a black pin on Tobruch in Lybia, our H.Q. was happy to pin a victory. Montgomery had stopped the enemy in El Alamein in Egypt. If the wind kept turning, we would need another kind of pin flags, some with a V painted on. The musical V for victory had been created in England at "Radio-Belgique," still in a kitchen of the BBC. De Laveleye, one of its members, had taken, as station signal, the first notes of the Beethoven's fifth symphony corresponding to the Morse transcription for V. Winston Churchill had made it visual with a finger sign for Victory.

Aggraver – Verschlimmerung – Worsen

Another shock came when Vichy France fell under the German control. No more France Libre (Free France). For my father's chain, it meant many more miles to cover with precaution. On the other hand, now we could send mail to our friends in Réalmont. I missed them so much; for so long we had been without news. In the first letter, they were slowly adjusting to the new regime and everybody was fine. Later on, sad news: Josette had died from her heart problem, impossible to be solved at that time. Even if it was expected, we were awfully sorry. Such a pleasant girl, such nice people in sorrow. We kept exchanging sporadic mail; the postal service was still irregular.

Right after, the part of the French Navy anchored in Toulon on the Mediterranean coast scuttled itself. To remember that act of courage, the first open act of resistance, we all bravely wore a little broach, which represented a French sailor's hat. We had patiently made it with a coin, an old twenty-five cent coin with a whole in the middle, covered with blue wool, a string of red, and a tiny white pompom.

The Gestapo got more repressive and cruel, as many acts of terrorism had popped up. One of Dad's friends had been arrested and forced to hang himself on a tree along the main road as an example.

A sneaky officer came a few times for inspections. To avoid the attention, he took the old model rail car, but the conductor, who knew his passengers, used a personal code to announce him. When they reached the hilltop, where it could be heard, he blew a few more "Toot . . . Toot . . ." than usual, enough to have the brigade ready to welcome the Pro. Dad had to show a little more enthusiasm in his job. So, in honor of the Clean and always Right Third Reich, he arrested two black market big wheels, as if he didn't know they were acquainted with German and Belgian "gestapists." It was like killing two birds with one stone. A few guys received a premature ticket to the Russian front.

The S.T.O.—obligatory working service in Germany—was now established for the men from eighteen to fifty and the women from twenty-one to thirty-five. So Dad would pass not only pilots and "specialists," but more and more youngsters who joined the new Belgian Army reborn in England with the Belgian Colonel Piron. They would be trained in Ireland. Many others found refuge in farms, castles, convents, presbyteries, and forests. The "Maquis" (from: to take to the bush) was born. The Maquis were Resistants that operated in the fields and forest doing whatever they could to sabotage the Germans.

Ceinture – Gurtel – Belt

The choice of food became more limited. Fortunately, we could supply ourselves with potatoes, beans, peas, and all kinds of fruits and vegetables growing in our garden and in plots my parents rented from some farmers. I don't know how Maman and Dad could find the time and the energy to do so, not only for us, but to share with the aunt who had four children and a small garden. I remember once, after a solid pea-shucking afternoon, every time I closed my eyes, all what I could see was: peas - peas - peas.

My little cousins Anne Marie and Ghislain, one at the time, came and spent some vacations with us. We had the privilege of living in the boondocks, away from the Allied bombing menace that had started on our territory.

Cible – Scheibe – Target

The planes were not yet equipped to perfectly locate their targets. It unfortunately happened that they took the moon reflection on a glass roof for a strategic point, which caused many victims, as their bombings could make everything turn into debris. Our history teacher lost her mother and her sister in a stupid accident: an empty barrel of gas, dropped from an American plane, fell on their chimney. The two ladies were cooking and both perished in the explosion. Fighting together for the same cause, people considered these damages as destiny. Resentment was reserved for the Germans and their acolytes.

Our school was not far from an industrial zone that became a problem again. Quite often sirens broke the rhythm of any work. Our nerves had to be strong.

As time went by, more pins had to be placed on courageous Stalingrad, so heavily bombed.

Meanwhile, our dear aunt Victoria, our former rallying point, died in Douai. Very sad that Dad was the only one to have the possibility of attending her burial. Due to travel restrictions, only immediate family could get a pass to attend a funeral.

Quarante-trois – Drei und viertzig – Forty-three
The year 1943 was at the door. In January, the Germans faced enormous problems in Russia, even with the Flemish Legion. Hitler had decided to merge them into a SS Division. Some of them, who had gone to fight communism, refused to become just killers. There were still some idealists.

As no marshal had ever given up, Hitler promoted Von Paulus to "save the marbles." Well, the next day, Marshal Von Paulus surrendered. That event put a balm on our hearts.

In February, on a sunny day, I turned fifteen. Back from school, I found a little cake on the kitchen table. A mocha cake with a pretty decoration to replace the no-more-existing candles. How had my mother been able to whip that surprise? For me it stayed, forever, THE unforgettably delicious birthday cake.

Soon after, we were ordered to bring to the City Hall: iron, copper, brass, nickel, and pewter, all that could be used to help the problematic replacement of the German Army's equipment. Even coins were converted to German equipment. They didn't claim too much, as everybody did hide and even buried the wanted items. They sure didn't get Dad's ruler! The fifty cent coins made out of nickel became arrogant jewelry pieces.

Courage – Mut – Courage

One of my uncles, Robert, who was a civil engineer in Brussels, was arrested. He had given the Allies the formula of the special concrete particularly used to build the Atlantic Wall defenses. He was in the prison Saint Léonard in Liège. A few days later, Hélène, his wife, my father's sister, met the same fate, leaving their daughter, Fernande, alone. She was sheltered by their neighbors, who informed Dad. It was easy to understand that it was dangerous for them to keep a terrorists' offspring. Even if our relationship was nonexistent for former family reasons, he had not visited the family since he married. Dad went to fetch her. She was almost seventeen and, in spite of the danger, rather reluctant to come stay in our village and leave her friends and boyfriend. She stayed with us over a month. One morning a passeur brought a note from her mother. Just a few words written on toilet paper — "I'm O.K. We never saw the lady who had coffee with us, hide the cow. Love." Puzzle!

My cousin fortunately remembered a lady who had come at their house, introducing herself as a friend and proposing her services to sneak in the Liège prison and carry some messages. Her mother had served some malt coffee with some milk in a little cow-shaped pot. Apparently something fishy was hidden there. The next morning at dawn, Dad pretended that a serious problem had happened in the family, and he took her to Brussels. They found the suspicious milk pot, buried it in the garden, and came back. After that, my cousin adopted the attitude shamelessly dangerous to invite people my parents didn't know and more. She often went out alone and had an unhealthty curiousity of my father's activities — we could not trust her discretion. Fernande wanted to be sent back to Brussels. Instead, Dad organized a hazardous trip to Revin, France deliver her to our grandparents who kept Fernande the remaining months her mother was in jail.

My Aunt Hélène came back in sad shape, with a kidney destroyed by the beatings she had endured during the interrogations under judicial torture, but she survived after laborious care. Strong lady, she felt like a victor; the Gestapo had not been able to get any information from her. At that time, still rebellious, she offered me an illegal cross made out of fifty-cent coins. I still have it. All Belgium coins had been converted to German paper money, so the metal could be used in the war effort.

Uncle Robert was later on killed in deportation during a bombing followed by a flood.

Mort – Todt – Death

The increasing bombing in Germany cost the life of fifty thousand citizens in Hamburg and one hundred thirty-five thousand in Dresden. When would we see the end?

In spite of his generals' advice, Hitler unleashed the operation "Citadelle-Festung Europa" in Kursk. It would be known as the largest armored battle in history. It failed. Germany lost the East.

Compliquer – Erschweren – Complicate

Our H.Q. could barely keep up with the events, chiefly because we couldn't meet so often anymore. School had increased the homework in spite of our long, difficult days. For many reasons, we lived with, in the back of our mind, the fear of possible disaster. We were tired.

Dad's chain was also more demanding. On top of the "passage" of people, he now had to organize the landing of a small plane that would bring some "specialists" with their materials and take some V.I.P back. To find a place for the plane to land had not been too difficult, as we lived at the edge of a plain. But to still be unnoticed when you have to assure the signal with lights around required more than imagination. With some partisans' help, it could be done. The passenger Dad had to bring to the plane was a chief of the Gestapo kidnapped in Liège.

Le pas – Der Schritt – The step
Our attention was glued to the German volley of blows in Russia. We could not keep track of all the parts of the world, except Italy, where Generals Patton and Montgomery's difficult progression in Sicily and, later on, in Italy itself, was anxiously followed step-by-step. Mussolini's arrest by his former German Allies marked a turn. Marshal Bodigliani took the reins. In our hearts, we gave Patton an extra star as he forced the surrender of the Africa Korps when our well-known Rommel had been called back to Berlin.

The Pacific Ocean sure didn't deserve its name anymore. USA, Australia, New Zealand, and Japan were fighting like mad. In the Far East too, it was good that the Allies had received some help from China, which had permitted an airlift over the Himalayas. Enough for us to run out of pins.

Erreur – Fehler – Mistake

One afternoon Léon Degrelle's secretary came to pay a visit. Very elegant, an elegance patterned on the Aryan look he had cleverly emphasized. As Mr. Pro, his role was purely political and had nothing to do with Dad's job, we thought it was a visit of courtesy. Mom and I, sitting in the room next to the office, would not miss anything of the event. To start in the mood of that sort of visit, Dad welcomed the visitor by his first name as he always did before, as he had known him since his was a child. His Majesty, arrogantly throwing his fine leather gloves on Dad's desk, answered, "I am Herr Ober Something and I am here to check what you are doing."

Maman and I had a look at each other: "Oh, oh." We remembered a certain iron ruler.

With a calm and unusual voice, we heard Dad saying, "Sorry, you don't have the ability to do so."

The other's voice reached a note higher: "I have the power to do what I want."

Dad, another note higher: "As far as my job is concerned, I have more power than you do, and your power, you should put it in your feet to move away from here as fast as you can. If not, my brigade will help you."

His Highness, pale with rage, took off, forgetting his gloves on the desk. At night, his father called Dad to ask him to bring the gloves back. He heard this answer: "The gloves will stay here until your son comes to fetch them himself."

As one says in the serials: To be continued.

Pélerin – Pilger – Pilgrim

During the performance at the office, the man on orderly duty was a gendarme called Pilgrim, a nickname earned in the defense of the 1940 invasion. The Pilgrim had a good time, silently giggling behind his papers. In 1940 some people caught in the middle of a battle could go crazy, but he had saved a lady who thought she was the Virgin Mary. She had fearlessly walked in front of the blazing guns to try to pacify the fighters. Jumping out of his trench, he had brought her back and convinced her he was a pilgrim in need of her help.

The Pilgrim was born in Binche, a city renowned for its carnival, chiefly for its Gilles' guild. From father to son, they had the privilege of performing a "rondeau" around the city main square dressed in strangely decorated costumes with little bells around their waists and ankles. For three days, after a solid breakfast composed of oysters and champagne, they danced in wooden shoes, carrying a basket, full of oranges they energetically threw at the crowd. For the rondeau, they wore a four-foot-high hat, an heirloom, made of the most expensive white ostrich feathers. Their lively and rhythmic music encouraged their enthusiastic followers to go on. Besides that, the Pélerin was a quiet and fatherly person.

The Pilgrim used his rondeau skills to save a few English officers, paymasters, blocked in the same trench as the "Virgin Mary." The Pilgrim had found the solution. Seeing a table in the wreckage of a nearby house, he ran to fetch it, jumped on it, and started to sing as loud as possible while dancing a frentic "Gilles" folk dance. The enemies, for sure, thought he was another crazy one. Instead of shooting at him, they shot at the table's feet to make him fall in the middle of laughs. The officers could escape with their money. One of them wanted to throw him some reward, but he refused: "No, I'm on the way to die soon." For sure, he had taken what Dad had also received, a gulp of ether their Commander gave his troops to keep them in line before a battle.

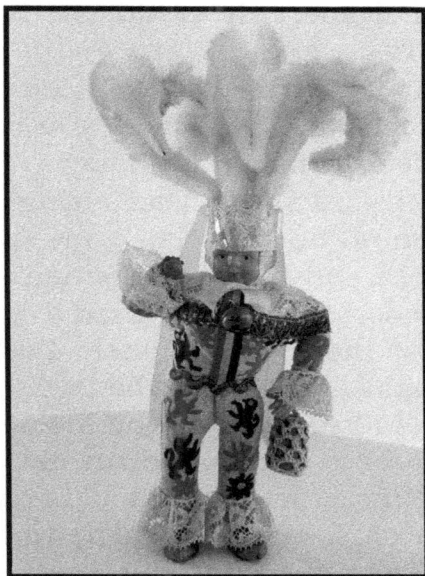

Souvenir de Binche - one Gille

Boomerang – Boomerang – Boomerang

The Resistance made more and more fruitful incursions: block army convoys, keep contact with the Allies and lots more. The Pros were rather nervous. Same reaction on the German side. The Gestapo arrested many people, tortured them, shot them to death. The Pro General had sent a note to order some gun practice in the brigades in case of possible terrorist attack. Dad sure had no worry about that menace, but he would play the game and practice the defense.

One day he heard, through the village tom-tom, that Herr Ober Something was boasting about the way he would fetch his gloves, he would come with a "Black

Brigade." He could not have picked a better time. The scene got prepared to welcome them. The paved courtyard in front of the office building was closed by a metallic fence; you could just see the arrivals' feet. When they noticed black boots and a pair of elegant shoes, Dad's men, well trained for the action, in no time fell flat, guns ready, on the ground taking the conventional position. Energetically pushing the door, the visitors faced a complete brigade who aimed at them. Immediately Dad ordered a "at ease." He apologized for the bad welcome due to an expected act of terrorism, and he insisted on the fact that he had luckily recognized an old acquaintance in time. No time to know if the old acquaintance believed in the excuse. Pale again, he ran out with his black gang. The gloves stayed in Dad's drawer as a war trophy.

Cachot – Kerker – Dungeon

A few German soldiers' groups on leave arrived. Some of them were in convalescence. After their dramatic experience on the Russian front, they were easy going. As our place had been an equestrian brigade, they found room for their horses. Among these warriors between difficult assignments were three Polish men who had been enrolled, against their will, in the German Army. All these men seemed fed up with the orders yelled out by a harsh officer who asked Dad for the keys to three dungeon cells and regularly filled them up with other unruly conscripts. They were rude with their recalcitrants, and they sometimes simply forgot to bring them their food.

Needless to say, these guys attracted our compassion. Maman made more soup that us kids, acrobatically, sneaked between the high-perched cell windows rods, on the condition they would say: "Hitler kaput." They never missed their soup. Dad found a more convenient way to help them. The recalcitrant group came out to clean the stable. Dad pretended that a terrorist menace was causing a lack of time to scrub the courtyard, and he proposed that the German chief put his rebels on this job as an additional punishment. The chief immediately accepted. Then Dad asked him for the keys. He promised to bring the prisoners back in himself after work, so it wouldn't disturb the military schedule. O.K.

The three Polish men took their sweet time to root the grass grown between the courtyard cobblestones. When the watch was a little loose, they carefully waited for a sign to let them run into the kitchen and find, every time, something to warm them up. Two of them spoke a German as broken as ours. We heard about their odyssey, their destroyed families. The third one, who never said a word, was just heaving sigh after sigh. As he had a flat emotionless face, the kids amiably called him: flat trap.

Cheval – Pferde – Horse

Once, an impeccable inspector came to check the camp. He even visited our rabbits' breeding hutch. Maman and I were feeding them. To be nice, he took a sprig of straw and offered it to a rabbit, which promptly turned its back. In perfect French, colored by a perfect German accent, with a straight face, he said, "So, you don't accept a present from a German officer?" He left Maman and me laughing in our sleeves.

The soldiers stayed a couple of months before

being sent to another front. They left a little horse they had brought from Russia. It had no name, no master, and it was more stubborn than a mule. No one knew the right words to make it move. It was a worn-out small horse, a type we call a "rosse" in French, so we gave that name a Russian consonance, we called it "Rossov." The best was done to train and feed it before the authorities would come and fetch it, but nobody came, and Rossov became a member of our community, fed like rabbits, with tons of grass.

Mixte – Gemischt – Mixed

That year the program offered by the school was reaching its end for me. To finish the last years before the baccalaureate (BAC), I would have to commute to Mons, over one hour away, by tramway and railway. With the mixed-up transportation and the increasing bombing, it was out of question.

In my school, the boys' section had a supplementary program. Our cousins were the director's friends; together, they arranged for me to join that last class. No problem. Since I was born, I only had boys around me: cousins, friends, neighbors. With them, I had been squaw, canteen stewardess, burglar, detective, assistant expert in forensic medicine on a poor doll, member of a bike-racing team, and more.

Well, I soon realized it could even be more interesting. For some of my twenty-eight schoolfellows, I was not only a partner but "a girl." I never had such help and escort. I became a specialist in science and algebra, but kept hating the basic calculus.

Sabotage – Sabotage – Sabotage

The Resistance, then, extended its actions. More military trains were derailed, more electric lines got cut, more gas containers exploded, so more hostages were taken and people arrested.

The former newspapers, severely censored, were still published. One morning "Le Soir" (the Evening) the most important publication, came out with the real news, not German propaganda. What a success!

The Chain lost a few links, but some written and oral messages still had to go. Commuting to school to Quiévrain every day, I could help. Fortunately, the persons we had to contact had their son in my school, so it would not look suspicious if I went to their place. Oral messages were always extremely short and easy to slip in the conversation. For instance: "Maman would like to know if you still have a—whatever?" For the written messages, it was more delicate.

As Dad had previously taken a subscription to the super-pro magazine "Signal" to look then like a sympathizer, he thought it would be good to make it useful. Signal, cleverly codified, became a messenger. In case of a patrol, I could say I brought the magazine to school to show the pupils how great Germany was. Fortunately, I was never in trouble. I had solid protection. When I started my partisan activity delivering oral messages, Dad slipped something in my pocket. It was my little Saint Benoît I had given him in 1940, saying, "He will protect you as he did for me."

With my little Saint Benoît, I delivered several messages each week as I went about my normal trips to school. Fortunately I was never stopped and questioned. My assignments were never too far from an easily explained location. The authorities underestimated a young school girl doing her part to help.

At this stage of the game, we all needed serious protection. I remember I always added a little prayer when passing in front of the church where Sainte Thérèse de Lisieux was in special favor. Sainte Thérèse had helped me survive an "in extremis" mastoidectomy surgery performed on a New Year's Eve when I was nine years old. Due to an extreme ear infection, they had made a four inch incision behind my right ear.

Plus - Mehr - More

Because of the links shortage due to many arrests, the Chain was in need of an operator for its broadcasting station. This sure was one of the most dangerous undertakings, as it never took long to be noticed and located. After searching many places where he could work it out, Dad alerted the English expert who came, by dinky plane, to teach him how to handle the station. Not only did our Englishman bring the material, but he also brought two assistants. They smoked their exotic cigarettes, which spread an unusual odor in a country where that kind of tobacco mixtures had disappeared for years. It took a solid ventilation to get rid of the smell, but the radio stayed at home. It needed to be carried to the next suitable post. Dad made the passage with that awkward packet on his bike. As we were relatively far from an equipped control center, Dad, fast operator and mover, was never caught.

CHAPTER EIGHT

Carefulness

Secret - Geheimhaltung - Secrecy

The controls by Germans and "Black" Belgians supporting the invaders were multiplied. People felt uneasy; they checked closer what was going around them. An old insomniac neighbor called the Pilgrim to share a secret with him. In her local dialect, she told him: "El Commandant, y fait l'fraude au nut, c' est que mi, d'je l'guigne" ("The commandant is smuggling at night, I keep a close watch on him.").

As if he had another secret for her, the Pélerin whispered, "Don't you ever repeat that to anybody because if, instead of smuggling, he was working for the resistants and they feel you're spying on him, you would be in deep trouble."

A few days before, the Resistance had robbed some black market dealers and killed two high-pros informers. Also, two other dealers' barns had been burned out, a show impossible to miss with such frightening heat, high flames, cracklings, and sparks. The insomniac chatterbox followed the advice. A letter addressed to the Gestapo, coming from the mother of a well-known lawyer, had been intercepted by the Underground. It was a list of names, the names of non-cooperators. Dad was on it. So a colleague who had closely followed her investigation watched this mother until the day she went herself to the Gestapo. A bullet had stopped her voyage. This time Dad's name was the first on the list rapidly removed from her bag.

Indésirable – Unerwunscht – Undesirable

A few days later, coming back from school, a cautious neighbor came up to me. She advised me to wait before going home, we had some visitors. A black car was parked conspicuously in front of our home. Immediately, I thought, O.K, at this time, Dad is not there and nobody knows what he is up to. Even so, Dad had very little knowledge; it was limited to his own responsibilities, and he knew no names of people he was working with. He also was too prudent to leave anything compromising around. The "Signal" was in my school bag. I kept trampling on the sidewalk for what seemed an eternity, until what looked like a flock of crows took off.

Not for a moment had I thought that Maman could have been involved in the process. I had pictured the Blacks searching in Dad's office, not at home. A shock! When I opened the door, I discovered the house upside down: all the closets were wide open, every item was on the floor, and, in the middle, Maman, who seemed like she was frozen in a state of petrification. She had a reddish complexion I never saw on her before. She explained that, when she saw the whole group exiting the office and coming toward the house, she had felt the blood leaving her face. As she didn't want them to think she was turning pale because she had something to hide and was afraid of them, she had rushed to the bathroom and quickly put on as much make-up as she could. Sure, she was not pale, but her eyes were still twice as round as usual. She was also recuperating from her worry about seeing me coming back in too soon. Then she had a look in the mirror, and we nervously burst out laughing.

When he came home, Dad didn't seem overmuch surprised; he was deeply relieved we were still together. Anyway, Maman and I were furious because of the mess they had left, chiefly me who, the night before, had sorted my books and papers and found now the work I had to turn in the next day covered with boot marks. The Gestapo had not found any tangible reason to come back. They had only closely checked a copy of a letter a young cousin had written to his mother before being shot to death. For us, we kept checking carefully on our emergency exit.

Style – Style – Style

Fortunately, school was rolling on wheels, as I said. The teachers were nice. We only had one semi-pro. The weekly hour we spent with him often turned out to be rather tense. We were still burying our cod liver oil capsules. We were surviving even if some of us still suffered from their 1940 injuries and family loss. If some were hungry, if some couldn't share their worries, we succeeded to make a solid group.

November 25, Sainte Catherine's Day, was the girls' day. My class offered me the funniest synthetic doll you can imagine. She had celluloid parts connected with string to balls that made the body. We had fun with anything we could find. We were ready for the adolescent world.

Maman suspicious of photographer

The music was turning into jazz, then "Swing" appeared. Next, everyone wanted to be a "Zazou." Fashions were changing. A Zazou boy had to let his hair grow to the bottom of his neck, wear a high collar white shirt, a curvy tie, a jacket down to his knees and narrow pants, short enough to show three inches of white socks. A Zazou girl wore a short skirt, one hand over the knee, a long jacket, white knee socks, and a hat with a square front rim, as high as possible; it had to be put on the back on a fluffy hair reaching the shoulders. The dream look.

For most of us, it stayed a dream. Our rationing tickets were not generous enough to replace a wardrobe. Moreover, our parents didn't applaud at that craziness. Most of them could not afford it and were not in the mood for these extravagances. With patience slowly turning into insistence, we succeeded to win the white socks. To compensate for the jacket length, Maman unraveled old items and re-knitted outsized outfits. She had plenty to do, as I was growing like a weed. The ersatz (substitute) material didn't work out. I remember the wool made out of rabbit hair; the items were so scratchy that, when taken off, your skin looked like a raspberry. One of Maman's friends, a tailor, made me a coat out of a dyed chestnut-brown blanket. With that, my elegant knitwear, and my hat coming from a Grandpa's former Borsalino, I felt like model of High Couture.

Suivre – Folgen – Follow

These fun distractions didn't keep us away from the developments of the war. The Russians were still fighting hard, and the Allies were blocked in Italy. The U.S. had destroyed a large part of the Japanese Navy at Midway and were also very active in the Philippines.

Here, as only ten percent of the recruited people by the S.T.O. had arrived in Germany, the "Blacks" were searching for the ninety percent of the others. The Underground Army, the Secret Army, helped the non-cooperators. They provided papers, military training, and if necessary, money they had robbed from dealers or, sometimes, from banks.

Revanche – Rache – Revenge

One morning in May 1943, my father received an official paper notifying him that, starting from the reception of this document, he was removed from his post. Motive: "Not fitting in the German establishment frame." For the Belgian establishment, he would be considered as inactive and would receive a third of his salary as a pension. We had a week to empty the house. We had expected something of that kind, and it was almost a relief to be aware of the verdict, which could have been drastic if Dad had been found – "La main dans le sac" (the hand in the bag), as we say.

Fortunately my grandparents in Havré had enough room to shelter us. Grandpa's ébénisterie workshop was far from being full; he had only kept one sculptor and one assistant. Their cabinet work consisted of repairs of antique furniture damaged by bombs or vandals or copies when the repair was impossible. Grandpa had also selected his customers. If he had the suspicion that their money came from a "black" activity, he pushed them away. He suddenly had no more adequate wood, no more glue, and so.

Cachette – Schlupfloch – Hide out

As soon as he knew the reason why we would come to their place, Grandpa could immediately foresee the possible problems, and he started to build a hideaway. One of the bedrooms could be connected to the wood reserve opening on the garden, close to a grove. Secretly Grandpa cut an opening just large enough to slip into a shelter that could hold three persons. One had to pass two zigzags behind a pile of boards to exit. From inside the room, one couldn't imagine the existence of that opening, well hidden under a piece of heavy furniture that would move easily if one knew the secret. An early OO7.

Dad had to disappear as soon as possible. As he had to quit, right now, he could be arrested for disobedience. Maman and I were expected to take care of the move. Moreover, Dad had to warn the Chain that he was burned here. Since the search at home of the investigative Gestapo, my parents had prepared an escape. Dad said a quick good-bye to his semi-puzzled men, put his bag on his bike, and left.

Deliberately, he took the direction of the border. He gave the news to the custom's agents he knew, and he pretended the only solution he had to get out of Belgian control was to go and live with his family in France. It was a little bit illegal, but they helped him out. Of course, the whole maneuver was a fake. Dad had to be back at night to finish his work. Once more he would imitate the owl's cry to signal his presence, tell the Chain that his cover was blown and that he needed another assignment. At dawn, wily Daddy came back home, bringing with him a most unpleasant smell. Poor Dad. A farmer had helped to take back, him and his bike, hidden in the straw of a carriage that had some pig's manure as co-passenger. After a good shower and a dinner, Dad left for good. A fast departure to camouflage worries and sadness.

Soon after, I heard repeated scratches at the door. I was scared but curious to know who was there.

Through the whisper coming from the keyhole, I recognized Jacques, a friend who had also been in flight for weeks. Maman turned the light off and let him in. He had a few messages for his resistants' chain, and he planned to say hello to his family next door.

The very next morning, the Gestapo arrived at their place. Jacques, his mother, and his sister, Nelly, were ready for lunch. When he saw a sinister black car slowing down, close to their home, Jacques immediately escaped through the garden bushes. His mother cleverly dropped his plate, glass, and silver in the deep soup boiler on the stove. When the visitors entered, she was just with her daughter. Old limping lady with an artist look, it seemed normal that she stayed on a chair quite close to the stove during the visit and even enjoyed to puff on a pipe, the pipe her son had forgotten in his flight. Normal too that she used two bedrooms because of her insomnia. The visitors left with empty hands. Then she could leave her strategic place. The whole time she had planned a trick in case that, if boiling, the soup would have let plates and silver make a dangerous noise. Later on, Jacques came back for a furtive good-bye.

Maman actively prepared the move helped by Dad's men, maybe Rossov and a rented large carriage. Two trips could be necessary. Fortunately, no Rossov was involved—we could get an official mover.

Coupure – Einschnitt – Cut

Dad's departure was hard on us. Also leaving the school on me. Because of our forced isolation, school was much more than a school, it was my entire social

The illegal nickel jewelry

life. The fact of going away at the end of the week did upset the people who presumed the reason why. As a sign of solidarity, the boys decided to disrupt the pro-teacher's class, the Germanic languages' master. He sensed what was going on. He noticed I wore, with bravado, my cross made out of illegal fifty-cent coins. Then he started, in a low voice, a long speech about certain people who, not following the rules established by the pure Aryan justice and humanity model, were destroying the victorious race's efforts. He slyly stopped in front of me, waiting for a comment. I found it in the Latin civilization and coldly told him, "Sic transit gloria mundi" (thus pass the glory of the world). Laughs! Saved by the bell.

At that time, one of our traditions was a poetry booklet in which our friends would write poems, more often doggerels, or draw something. I just had time to pass it to four of them, who put nice souvenirs. My favorite escort even offered me his memorial broach representing a Zazou.

Cacher – Bedecken – Hide

Dad started to live like a vagrant; he stayed a few days at the time with some family members, in safe places or where he was needed. And he was more than needed, as an increasing number of links were missing in the chain. His prolonged activity consisted to another work with, the intelligence service MARC. At that time, he would protect the groups that perpetuated sabotages as well as supervise the parachuting and arms landing, and transfer them to whoever needed them.

These details were revealed much later. At that time, to divulge them would have worked like Nobel's famous discovery.

Dad's visits at home were so rare that once, in a dream, I saw him jumping like a frog from one water-lily to another. Maman, under physical and emotional pressure, was tired when we arrived in Havré.

We unpacked a minimum; we hoped our stay would be on a temporary basis. To avoid any inopportune curiosity, we gave, as a reason for our move, that Dad had taken his pension, which could be done after twenty years of service. For his back-and-forth moves, they were due to his difficulty in adjusting to civilian life. To keep himself busy, he could visit reachable distant family and friends he hadn't had the opportunity to see when he was working. For Maman too it was understandable to be here, as Grandma

had suffered a new severe attack of rheumatism and
needed some help.

Continuer – Fortsetzen – Carry on

To complete the picture, I needed a school. Mons
was the only city at an easy reach; it took twenty
minutes by a more modern but still overcrowded rail
car's service. The problem was to find a school that
would accept a pupil in the middle of a term without
asking too many inconvenient questions. Maman
knew the high school director, who had been her
teacher during W.W.I. So we went there. The lady
received us nicely. A few papers had to be filled out.
When Maman answered her questions about Dad's job
before his retirement, she darted an understanding,

*The school goodbye with
the Zazou*

pensive glance at us. Her daughter had recently been tortured and shot to death by the Nazis. I could start school the next Monday.

In Havré, we had to register at the, fortunately, not too curious City Hall. We got our new papers and the necessary tickets. For his "excursions," Dad received from the Chain a real identification card (stolen in the Kommandantur). To avoid any wrong reaction in an emergency situation, they had kept his first name, and his family name still started with a B. His new profession made us hold our sides laughing: he was a salesman in hosiery. Poor Dad, who couldn't recognize silk from flannel. A solid training was necessary. To add a professional touch, he was also given a briefcase with samples and an order book with the label of a company, sympathetic, of course.

My new class was rather small, but the teachers were distant. The atmosphere was totally different from what I knew. Soon I felt out of place among the sixteen girls, most of them snobbish "nouveau-riche." Their preoccupations were chiefly: curls, outfits, make-up, parties in their private clubs, nothing I could be interested in. To console myself, and the events speeding up, I thought it wouldn't be long before a change. The classes were more often disturbed by air-raid warnings and runs to the shelter. Back home, I missed our H.Q. I felt lonely when sticking the pins on my map.

Tactique – Taktik – Tactics

As the region had a few strategic points, the building of private shelters became highly recommended. My grandparents had a large garden to do so. Grandpa

Dad hosiery salesman

drew a well-thought-out plan. The shelter would be spacious enough to contain benches, water reserves, some food, medical kit, scoops, blankets, and our gas masks. The famous gas mask wore only once, when tried on. The shelter would be built in a place out of the eventual wreckage of the house. It would have two entrances in zigzag to avoid the outburst, and it would be deep enough, well, a mini Siegfried Line. Grandpa, Dad on passage, a neighbor, and two woodworkers dug and carried away soil and stones. Later on, we had, a few times, the opportunity to enjoy the comfort of the place.

The harassed Germans became much more nervous. Many more controls went on. On the road to Mons, a sanatorium located in the middle of the forest became suspected of protecting peculiar patients. So quite often, a patrol of men dressed in long, black leather coats stopped the tramway and meticulously checked the papers, the bags, and even the pockets. Dad was reassured of his papers' authenticity after a light search and no questions about hosiery.

All these difficulties and the Mons train station totally destroyed by Allied bombing shortened the school term.

Ami – Freund – Friend

On vacations again. Dad's ex-colleague's children came home too. They lived in the gendarmerie located in front of my grandparents' home. They were aged between ten to nineteen, three daughters and one son. They were witty and funny. The youngest girl, Thérèse, was a smiley bowl of curly blond hair; the second, Cécile, a brunette passionate about music;

the third, dark-haired Odile, a specialist in herb tea. The blond son had a stiff leg from a bad fracture due to a hasty exit to evade Gestapo control. His first name, a very out-of-style name, Isidore, always lively and energetic despite his stodgy name. The evenings would be livelier.

I just had to cross the street to play ping-pong with them until curfew. Good musicians, they played piano and we sang a lot, from Boy Scout tunes, and a WWI repertory that included "The Roses of Picardy," proper songs. Their parents were very nice, however conventional. My friends, a few family members, and my lovely mother and grandparents were a big help to support the worries brought by our "Traveler."

Tourner – Drehen – Turn

We felt closer to victory when the Allies started to move in Italy in 1944. At last, Monte Cassino was free after two hundred planes had bombed it. Then Rome was liberated. Well, it wasn't finished yet. Mussolini, escaped from Germany, had founded a new state in North Italy.

The British lost a naval battle in the East, and the Russians opened three fronts. For the Far East, we prepared flags for Guam. I say WE, as the whole family had joined me in the map's decoration. While shopping, we met one of Maman's friends. She was a widow, recently back with her mother. Her son had been caught and sent to work in Germany. She had spent WW I in England and still spoke English fluently. Aware of the school's problems, she proposed to give me some lessons. Wonderful! I had found a teacher. Totally illegal, but why not? English was verboten by the Germans. Lessons went for just a few weeks before a new, drastic change happened, anyway, long enough to convince me it was possible to learn that peculiar language you never knew how to pronounce or how to spell.

Bricoler – Brikolieren – Do it yourself

Between the bombings and war complications domestic life was going on. Maman had to be more imaginative than ever to fill the plates. Fortunately, we had a big garden around the shelter. The amount of food per ticket went down and was not always available. More ersatz products were on the market. Honey had been replaced with an artificial syrup that pretended to taste like honey. Vanilla smelled like medicine. Once Maman bought an expensive bar of chocolate which, melted, looked like a mustard plaster and tasted like it too. What Maman was missing the most was the coffee. For her birthday, I broke my piggy bank and offered her an actual $12 gift: a tiny envelope with twenty coffee beans.

Grandma never showed her pain, but her hands slowly became completely deformed. She was a cross-stitching fan, and she courageously kept it on. The unavailability of canvas didn't stop her—she used burlap. For the yarn, she took scraps from on-knitted items according to which she composed her patterns. She made, still-existing, beautiful works.

Leather also was out of common use. Our neighbor fabricated what she called "El sac ed bo" (the wooden bag). It was cleverly thought out. You needed two wooden rectangles and a narrower one for the base, a dozen of thin strips for the lid. The gusseted sides

Grandma Catherine's industrious piece of art on burlap

were made out of any kind of material you could find: cotton, wool, whatever. The wood was perforated to be attached to the fabric. The thin strips put on the fabric made the top flexible. For the wood, it could be painted or burned. Maman and I made two of them. Grandpa had prepared the wood. As he still had some old scraps from leathered chairs, the result was pretty elegant. So could be the shoes, which had high wooden soles easily worn out. To protect them, I made use of Grandpa's services again. We artfully ornamented these blocks with decorative nails.

At that time, payments could be barter: garden harvest, clothes, tickets, or cans of fish.

The Belgian coast had recently been invaded by a plethora of herrings, immediately legally fished and preserved. This was the first time we had fish since the war had started. We received it in a light tomato sauce: a one kilo can per person. A delight for me, but a present a bit excessive for large families when it did store very well.

Amer – Schmerzlich – Bitter

According to the BBC's messages, we knew something would come up very soon, but where and when? For several months, the Allies had organized the "Operation Fortitude" that disconcerted the Germans. It had succeeded in making them believe a landing would take place near Calais. Hitler was more nervous. From his bunker in Germany, he had decided, by himself, what had to be done.

Too bad for Rundstedt and for Rommel, with their unfinished Atlantic Wall. Too bad for Donitz and his boats, Goring and his planes. Himmler and his SS, actually the only ones still in good shape. Troops were moving around and didn't look like the greatest fighters they had been. The Gestapo still was. They came to clean the end of our street and arrested two men we knew. Visiting Dad, Maman, and I inaugurated the "hideaway for three."

Fabuleux – Fabelhaft – Fabulous

Early morning on the sixth of June 1944, we heard the so-long-expected news. THEY had landed! Everyone went crazy. We were not sure who to believe. According to an optimistic viewpoint, THEY would be here in a few days. In the official radio's opinion, IT would be under control in no time. Worries of facing the Germans' revenge came right afterward. They could stop transportation, cut electricity, even poison the wells. I don't know why water suddenly became the MUST. The drugstores were promptly emptied of the products to keep it drinkable. Everyone filled bottles, pots, and buckets. I never pumped so much water in my life. The same evening, through heavier static, the BBC announced the participation in the landing of four thousand five hundred boats and two thousand Allies planes on the Normandy coast. Twenty thousand paratroopers had been dropped, the Americans in Sainte-Mère-l'Eglise, the British in Ranville. The BBC branch "Radio Belgique" added that twelve hundred Belgians were incorporated in the British Royal Air Force (R.A.F.). The next day, the seventh of June, with two groups of twelve hundred men, including five hundred Luxembourgers plus five hundred vehicles, the Belgian Colonel Piron landed in Normandy.

We could prepare more pin flags for our map and huge flags for the windows. For these, we would keep them hidden for a while. It seemed that, like trapped game, the Germans were defending themselves with teeth and claws.

The Allies' move became problematic. Here the chain was reduced to a minimum, and many links were arrested. Dad had to be very careful, not only because of the Gestapo, which was more active, but some last-minute resistants' groups wanted to enforce their own action to be recognized as heroes. They were dangerous, as their lack of knowledge and organization put the real Resistance in real trouble.

One night, a fearless helper ran down the street, ringing at every door, claiming "Take off, a storage tank at Solvay, a few blocks away, will be blown up in fifteen minutes." Even if we had trained ourselves to reach our shelter in a few minutes, to be farther away in such a short time was impossible. Grandma was a slow mover and, in spite of her willingness to sacrifice, we would not leave her alone. We did our best. We were barely at the end of the garden when the huge tank, whose content we did not know, imploded with a frightening noise, it projected enormous flames, followed by the heaviest possible black smoke. The smell was unbearable, so, with our prepared wet towels on our noses, we went back home.

One could judge that this sabotage had been conducted by professionals. Only one tank was destroyed. The smoke was rising straight up because the wind had turned one hour before. So no problem for the surroundings. Right afterward, the police and a few ambulances arrived. Fortunately, no one was injured, not even the neutralized German guards. Then came the firemen and, of course, the Gestapo.

This time again, the three of us spent a few hours in the hideaway, counting the bullets hitting the tiles and waiting for calm to return. My grandparents went to bed; they pretended they were too old to be considered terrorists.

Punition – Strafe – Punishment

At the same time, another Underground Army link started to punish the active pros who had given people away to the Gestapo. A big wheel in industry was killed, so was our post-office director, in his office, one block away from us. The Germans reacted cruelly. They came in waves and took hostages.

The hideaway was fine, but not for too long. Dad and our next neighbor left for a farm located ten miles away in Gottignies, a village so small that, joking about a nowhere place, you would call it "Ene hamia d'Gotnie"—a hamlet of tiny Gottignies. Even there, once, they were forced to hide in a hay pile.

Our neighbor was a funny character. The lazybones prototype. He didn't mind the war because you didn't have to keep working while air raid warnings were on. Once, one of his colleagues had found him asleep in his mini-cloakroom. At the farm, he stayed so long in the hay that everybody worried about him. He came out when the work was almost finished.

He and Dad came back four days later. Life was normal (!) again.

Then we had the pleasure of sticking a few victorious flags on Normandy. Things were moving on in the Cotentin region, the harbor in Cherbourg, and the city of Caen. The Germans held high ground in the Falaise area which allowed them to slow down the Allied progression enough to evacuate their troops. The fighting caused many casualties on both sides and also among the civilians caught in the middle of them.

Tentative – Versuch – Attempt

On July 20, our feelings were split in two. On one hand, what a relief to hear that Germany had had enough of the war. Some high-grade officers had tried to kill their führer in his H.Q. The bomb had been placed by Colonel Count Claus von Stauffenberg. Sympathizer Stupnagel, even the German Commander in France, had already arrested a few Nazi chiefs. On the other hand, we worried when we heard that the devil had escaped. Knowing Hitler and his bloody craziness, the plot would cost many lives. Effectively, soon after, hundreds of concerned people were murdered or committed suicide to avoid torture. Their families also were executed. Our Rommel attracted our sympathy when we learned he had poisoned himself, saving his wife and their son from death. We tried to get more news from the neutral radio Genève channel in Switzerland. "Aqui Radio Andorra" in the little Principality in the Pyrenees was an odd nest of Spanish laws and French Bishop influences.

Résidu – Nachlass – Residue

To reinforce its army, Germany enrolled sixteen-year-old youngsters. Their size didn't matter which brought this comment: "If they cut their soldiers in two, we're not about to see the last of them."

They looked rather sad in their baggy uniforms. Insecure, not seriously prepared, sometimes scared, they were dangerous—they easily used their guns.

Russia signed the armistice with Finland and Romania changed camps. In the beginning of August, the Russians approached Warsaw, and the Germans counter-attacked. The inhabitants started a revolt, but the tired Russian Army couldn't help them. The German siege of Warsaw took three months for the Germans to prevail. By then, Warsaw was almost completely demolished and had lost two hundred thousand of its inhabitants.

Représailles – Wiedervergeltung – Reprisals

From the fifteenth of August on, every two days our family had a celebration. On the fifteenth, it was the Assumption, Holy Mary's feast, on the seventeenth my cousin Gérard's birthday, on the nineteenth Grandpa's birthday, and on the twenty-first my cousin Michel's birthday.

This fifteenth brought reassuring news. The Allies

*Over 140 young men were tortured and died
in the Maquis of Revin, France*

had landed in South France. How were our Réalmont friends doing? We hadn't received letters for ages. In France, their underground Army had, of course, the same mission as here. Their much larger country had huge forests to shelter their Maquis and thus had been engaged in many more fights, causing numerous victims.

In Revin, where my paternal grandparents lived, the Germans had found 140 local young men that they had tortured and massacred after making them dig their own graves. Uncle Maurice was saved; bringing the young men food, he had noticed suspicious tracks in his path and turned back. More to the south, in the "le Vercors" region, the largest massif of the French pre-Alps, it was the same drama. Except at the Grotte de Luire, Vassieux en Vercors and the third one named

Oradour-sur-Glanes, the entire population, not just the young men, had been burned, all inhabitants and buildings included. You never knew what to expect.

Remous – Wirbel – Stir

Meanwhile, Paris was liberated. The city was in a joyful effervescence, hailing the Allies, the Underground, the General Leclerc's Second Division, and the General de Gaulle, so much respected and admired.

Here in Havré, the Gestapo was still filling the jails and sending prisoners to Germany.

Some better news came from South France. The Allies and the French General de Lattre de Tassigny's division were pushing their way toward Dijon and later on to Alsace. From Normandy, the Allies could finally get out of their traps. The landing on the beaches— Sword, Juno, Gold, the difficult Omaha and Utah— had cost them two hundred thousand casualties and three hundred thousand on the German side. In May, Generals Eisenhower and Montgomery found a solution to quickly end this nightmare.

Some Allies and the General Leclerc's Second D.B. (Division Blindée) tanks were now heading towards Strasbourg. Later on to Bertchesgaden, after they had crossed the famous and still-active Siegfried Line, the Germans' last desperate defense. Meanwhile, a friend of ours, who was a volunteer in the 2nd D.B. lost a leg, injured in his tank during the attack on Strasbourg.

CHAPTER NINE
HURRA(H)! Liberation in Sight

Generals Bradley and Patton are moving their divisions in our direction.

One morning we heard that Patton's men had reached our region. Total enthusiasm!

Prévoyance – Vorsicht – Foresight

Grandpa Arnold, with his practical sense, thought that once more, confusion would set in for a while. So, as he had to go to the bank, he should do it right now. Well, the bank was in Mons, five miles away, without transportation. So what? He would walk. He had to cross the forest where some remnants of German divisions were anxious to regroup. They had opened a camp there two days ago. If Dad was here, maybe he could convince Grandpa of the danger, but Arnold just said, "Don't worry. They have more urgent business than to pay attention to a little old grandpa."

Then he left, leaving us in terror until his return.

He came back late afternoon, happy and bringing joyful news. As he had foreseen, no one had paid attention to him in the forest. The soldiers were preparing their defense. Downtown, people were excited, as one could hear the American tanks at a short distance. From some high points, one could even see some convoys. The bank was still open, so the trip was worthwhile. Grandpa had taken the time to have a quick beer (0.8 percent) in a café, and glean more information, but it was time to move. The Americans were less than two miles away from the Grand Place where he was. Fortunately, they stopped to secure their way over the canal and around the city.

As they were so close and the Germans waiting in the forest, the way back could be problematic, but when Grandpa arrived at the forest edge, he noticed there were no more guns. He kept walking. Not a soul. The soldiers' departure had surely been done in a panic, as there was still some laundry hanging and the dough for their bread was spread out on the path. A few people were already there with buckets to fetch some dough, a bargain for their "Adolph." They were amazed that Grandpa had the nerve to go to Mons. After a short chat and he rushed home. We were we relieved to see him back, and happily excited by the good news.

Fuir – Flien – Flee

Here, the day had been busy too. For hours, the German forest fugitives had crossed the city. I'll never forget one of the last ones I saw, the last of the convoy. He was an early-twenty tall blond on his horse holding, with difficulty, four other horses that had lost their riders. He was moving as fast as he could. He had lost his helmet, his face was as red as a beet, his eyes full of panic, he constantly checked the road behind him. The Underground Army had come out. Their objective was to push the Germans out of the area to avoid a slaughter. It would be easier to encircle them in the countryside over the canal. Some of the runaways were still tough; they hid anywhere, ready for a fight.

Retour – Herweg – Return

Dad came home, to our relief. He looked exhausted and simply said, "Mission accomplished."

The same night the hidden guys came out and started to shout at random. We couldn't use our garden shelter, as we suspected some of the fighters could be hiding there. My grandparents insisted that we run once more into the hideaway; as for them, they would stay in bed and, again, take a chance. We still counted a few bullets hitting the tiles. At dawn, the Underground Army came to the rescue; the calm was apparently back. Coming out of our hole, I peeped outside: horror, a German soldier, with his machine gun, was crawling along the side of the house. Dad, who had joined me, made some signs to keep me quiet and not worry. I never saw before the gun Dad was pointing at the soldier. In my ear he whispered, "It's just in case, he will be stopped soon."

Right. One block farther, the German solider was grabbed, to be, later on, put in a brand-new prisoner camp. By the way, we had been right not to use our garden shelter—we found cartridges all around it.

Ils sont ici – Sie sind hier – Here they are

Now, we had to actively prepare our decorations for THEIR arrival. We took the homemade flags out of their hideaway and started sewing blue, white, red, black, and yellow ribbons on the sleeves of our shirts and blouses. Why there? Because the few Germans left, whose reaction we feared, couldn't see them under a jacket, and we would be ready in no time for the Great Welcome. Hearing the heavy noise of a convoy, we rushed to put the flags up. "Oh, OH! Put them down, it's a German tank division." It happened a few times during forenoon, ups and downs, jacket off, jacket on. We crossed the street; we needed to gather news at our friends' place in the gendarmerie.

Wonderful! The Americans were coming out of the forest. The cleaned-out city could be crossed in less than an hour. Everybody was quite excited. While we were talking, a few shots rang out down the street. There were the "half-portion" leftovers who had escaped the night before. Obviously, they weren't aware of the rapid developments, or they didn't want to believe it.

Suddenly the last bells left in the church started a joyous carillon. THEY were there! Not even a mile away. The adolescent soldiers understood it was the end of their adventure, and they dropped their guns. They came close to the gendarmerie, most of them sniffing some tears, and they surrendered.

We went back home, put the flags up, and took our jackets off again. We were ready. Grandma was once more unable to stay too long on her feet. Grandpa brought her chair at the door; she didn't want to miss any detail of this historical moment. Many people were already on the sidewalks. Some armed Resistants were keeping a vigilant eye on windows and roofs. We were anxiously watching the top of our street. The owner of the house at the crest of the hill, a calm and serious accountat, was in front of his house suddenly jumping and waving like a cartoon character. No doubt, THEY were there.

They arrived, four in a jeep, followed at a distance by another group. Four smiling guys in more casual uniforms than the ones we were used to seeing. Their jeep was covered with flowers, bottles of wine saved for years for this occasion. They could barely hold their guns. Everybody wanted to touch them, shake hands with them. They were moving extremely slowly, and it seemed they had given up the idea to do anything differently. They had to go through thanks, laughs, tears of joy, and the only song we knew in English, learned through our parents' epic memories, maybe not the most appropriate: "It's a long way to Tipperary." Oh! Happy fourth of September 1944!

A few minutes later, a loudmouth strong woman, her apron on, arrived with a piteous German officer she was poking with a fork. She had found him in her garden shelter. She was proud, and some explanations were needed before she could admit that the Americans in their jeeps could not take him as a gift.

I was in the gendarmerie's hall when some "New Resistance" elements brought in an SS officer. Inexperienced, they looked at his revolver, not paying too much attention to him when he jumped like a tiger, took the arm out of their hands and put a bullet in his knee-cap. Faithful to his SS law which was only when wounded, did you allow yourself to be captured. Good, he didn't get to continue more SS cruel intentions, his war was over.

Surprise – Verwunderung – Surprise

The next day, heavy convoys went on, still well acclaimed. As they sometimes slowed down, we had time to offer them drinks and they offered us cigarettes. Packages we never saw before: Camels, Lucky Strikes, packed by five. Chocolate came later, when they stopped longer. Suddenly, a soldier stuck his head out of a truck and said in Walloon "Bondjou a tertous" ("Hello, everybody").

Surprise! Someone asked him "Vo ste d'par ci" ("Are you from around here")?

"Ed su americain. Dj'ai appris ave m'Grandme qui n'dvise co qu'el Wallon d' Thieu. D'ju ve du Wisconsin ou branmin des d'gins parl'te co Wallon." ("I am American. I learned with my Grandma who only speaks the Walloon from Thieu. I'm coming from Wisconsin where many people still speak Walloon.")

Thieu was a village just a couple of miles away. Oh, interesting, but where is Wisconsin? The truck took off. All we could do was to wish good luck to the young soldier and hope he could go home soon and tell his grandma he successfully used her language when crossing her home country.

Later at night, the radio announced that, on the third and fourth, Brussels had been liberated by the Welsh, the Irish, and the Belgian Piron's brigade. The Resistance had also been a big help. We learned that King Léopold III and his family had been discreetly transferred to Germany in June. Where?

For a few days, the German Army had beaten a general retreat. Some isolated units, not disposed to give up, had fought in a few places downtown: Avenue Louise, Place du Trône, even in the Parc

Here they are! Some thirsty Gis on their way to victory
- Irène and Gis

Tangible thank you

du Cinquantenaire, causing casualties among the Resistants. They also had burned the archives in the Palais de Justice, and mined the cupola, which had come down in flames.

In Antwerp, all the resistance services and a British secret service succeeded in protecting the harbor from a well-prepared German plan for flood and destruction. Some fights were still on in spite of the German commander's surrender. Anyway, the canals were getting cleared of their numerous mines without too much damage. The harbor would soon be ready to forward the Allies' material and, later on, the Belgian food supplies.

Renaissance – Wiedergeburt – Rebirth

Dad was a little more relaxed. The chain had communicated the procedure to prepare his governmental recognition, witnesses to contact, and more. This way, we learned that Dad was one of the two survivors of the whole chain. Terrifying, isn't it? His former officers sent him his reinstatement in his job. He was supposed to go back to Roisin before his promotion. Dad hoped all the pros would be sent to Sterpenich. Another family joke: Sterpenich was a nowhere place on the Luxembourger border where my father always threatened to send any slackers on his team.

The Belgian government, back from London, got formed after it had regrouped its members who had escaped from Vichy. They prepared the legal institutions' re-establishment. Because of the Belgian liberation's speed, nothing was yet in place and, controlling the new Resistants, who had given themselves the right to arrest and judge, was difficult. Many minor pros had already been molested, some killed, but the big wheels had time to take off. The women who had German boyfriends were shaved and insulted. The mob rage was dangerous. Dad was outraged—that was not what he had fought for. Then I realized how tired he was, how much weight he had lost, so had Maman. It was time to use this break to make plans and REST. We didn't remember a whole night's sleep.

The American troops were still going by, day and night. In spite of secrecy, the tom-tom announced that two generals were in the next convoy. That's how I got the opportunity and the honor to shake hands with generals Bradley and Patton. WOW!

The war was far from its end. The radio talked about "flying bombs" that had already attacked London. They were called V1 rockets, first letter for Vergeltungswaffe—reprisal arms. For us, it was far away and we were free, we felt invulnerable. We had to live again.

Pensionnat – Internat – Boarding School

Most families' first concern was their children's education. It was not the easiest problem to solve, as many buildings had suffered war damage. Most of the high schools around us could just manage to offer one class, the BAC terminal, the Baccalaureate exams. After my chaotic attendance, I still had some grades to finish.

The Enfant Jésus in Nivelles, thirty miles away, was the only one able to handle these classes. It was a large boarding school highly recommended by my two aunts who had studied there. The large building was well located on a hill with a huge park, which had been converted into a garden like everywhere else. The teachers were nice, the pupils pleasant. Some black points anyway: the mandatory, old-style black uniform. As none of us, at the time, could provide a brand new wardrobe, as we had items from different fabrics that didn't all dye the same way. We were teasing each other about our light or dark shades of black.

Then, in spite of the lack of heat and proper diet, we got up at 5 a.m. to attend mass and spend one hour of study where everybody was snoozing. The mail, to our parents only, was read by the director before it was sent, and so were the replies. Once a week, two by two, we could go for a well-guarded walk near the city center. As I needed a vaccination shot, Maman had to call one of her girlfriends who lived in Nivelles to accompany me; a Sister could not come into a male doctor's office and, no way, could I go alone. After the four active years I went through, being dropped into a close-minded society was a little puzzling, but it would only be for two years. I had seen worse.

Except for the food. The kitchen was still in total chaos. Not only was the food sparse, but it was poorly prepared. At 10 a.m., while we received a bowl of warm brownish liquid, we could see the large salad bowls already on the tables with, on top, a thick sauce smelling strangely like mustard plaster, tasting like it too at the 1 p.m. lunch. Our two ounces of meat, every single day, consisted of a lukewarm piece of lard placed on boiled potatoes. The two tablespoons of veggies were burned most of the time. You could buy a supplement of bread, at a high price. We were allowed only a five minute controlled deep bath or shower and that sucked away a lot of our money to the nuns. I understood why a disrespectful Walloon dictum said, "If your chimney air shaft doesn't work anymore, put a nun at the top." Girls of our age could have fun anyway; most of the time all this pettiness made us laugh. Fortunately, the study program was very interesting.

We were more or less aware of the last news. We knew some English, Polish, and American paratroopers had serious difficulties in Arnhem on the Rhine bridges and in Grave on the River Meuse. The English divisions that had left from Belgium had been caught in a tremendous battle that had caused a few thousand casualties. They had surrendered in Arnhem. Worries were not over.

Although we couldn't go home more than once every trimester, we could receive some visits, once a month, on Sundays. The transportation was still problematic, Army first. Maman took a train that dropped her in Manage; from there a rail car was supposed to take the relay. Not that day, because of an electricity shortage. So Maman walked the last five miles, carrying two heavy suitcases packed with sheets and warm clothes. She had read between the lines of my censored letters. She also had brought some food, saving her war cookies in a tin box to protect them from the mouse running in my cabinet. She also had added the most welcome rabbit "delicacies" preserved in glass jars. Poor Mom, she arrived exhausted, and she seemed a little surprised to be shut up in a parlor. We were so happy to be together that it didn't prevent us from talking and talking. Maman was anxious to know how I was doing, and I was anxious to know how they were doing at home. Here, my extra lessons in the boys' school had put me ahead in science and math. The teacher had advised me to change over the science section because they needed math teachers. Hating calculus, I didn't feel "made out of the wood you make math teachers with," as they say here. I had preferred to stay in my "letters" section. Maman agreed with it.

At home, the whole family was doing fine. Dad had started to work again; he was happy. Their move back to Roisin was fixed for the following week. Grandma was much better, and Grandpa had reopened his entire workshop. Maman, who had to go back the same way she had come, had to leave. Fortunately, the suitcases were not so heavy anymore, just a load of laundry.

When she left I saw in her eyes a dubious opinion about the place, but she looked relieved, so I could cope with it.

Encore – Immer Noch – Still

Insecurity was back. V1 were attacking more often on our territory. We learned how to recognize them. If you heard "toc, toc, toc . . ." no worry, they were going farther. If the sound stopped on top of your head, too bad, but your worries would be over forever. Later on the V2 were more dangerous, as you couldn't hear anything. Every time an air raid warning sounded, we went back to the routine of rushing into the shelter without the feeling of a direct menace.

The British Army decided to reopen the military airport near our place. The R.A.F. pilots would be quartered in our school. They would occupy the top floor. Poor Sisters! We guessed they thought about barbed wiring each of us. After a few days of hammering planks and burlap on some passages, the pilots took up their quarters as discretely as possible. The change on our side was noticeable through the heavy smell of their cigarettes, largely compensated for by a much-appreciated gift. That night we had some "spam" for dinner. Not too long after, the presence of our co-habitants attracted V1 like flies around honey.

For the eleventh of November, our Veterans' Day, we did prepare songs and decorations for a solemn Mass in memory of all the war casualties. After all these ups and downs, we were tired. The same night

I was awakened by an extremely anxious Sister. She nervously repeated, "How are you? How are you?"

I still wondered why she intruded in my sleep when I noticed there were broken windows in the hall behind her. I was sleeping so deeply that I didn't hear the bombing. I grabbed clothes, shoes, and the inseparable bag with my official papers before we carefully rushed down to the shelter. The way was paved with pieces of glass and debris. There was a deep relief sigh when we came in. The Sister could not make them believe she had found me sound asleep. The director started a rosary, which calmed down the excitement and put everyone into a snooze like magic. Eight other V1 fell in our area that night, but we did not suffer from them.

Départ – Weggang – Departure

The next morning the authorities closed the schools again. We had to leave "as soon as possible," an order that was just a wishful thinking. We could not call for help, no telephone. Foreseeing the limited space we would find in a train, we could only take one suitcase, and leave behind us, books, linen, mattresses, and the rest. The poor Sisters gave up on watching us, they opened the broken cage of their home— that they had to make livable again before night. A quick good-bye and we walked to the train station, barely able to carry our overloaded suitcases. There we met dozens of students from the other schools. The railway was organizing extra trains between the military convoys. It took a while before we could embark, packed like sardines. We were stopped ten miles farther as the line had been destroyed by some other V1. Then rail cars took the relay. A few hours later we had only moved six miles away—no hope of reaching home in Roisin that night. Blocked in La Louvière, not too far from Havré, I looked for another rail car line. At the stop, in the crowd, I met a student whose parents lived on the same street my grandparents did. Once more we were pushed inside like in the Tokyo subway. Good he was there! He helped me to find my suitcase, which had been propelled on the other side of the car.

We arrived in Havré at almost 10 p.m. Because of a lack of electricity, the rail car dropped us at the bottom of our street. We were tired, as our breakfast was far behind us. We were the only ones on the street. At that stage of the game, we considered the situation as a gag, and we burst out laughing, which didn't help us to push our monstrous suitcases uphill.

We were still laughing when Grandpa opened the door, wondering who could be at the door at this unusual time. First, Grandpa seemed turned into a huge question mark, followed by a relief sigh. Grandma arrived, she exclaimed "Mon!" (My!), with the local modulation meaning an exclamation mark. The radio had announced the bombing with the detail there had been no casualties. They were happy to see us. Just a little chat on the doorstep and my companion of adventure left. He was eager to go home and reassure his parents too. I was filthy, thirsty, starving, and, most of all, exhausted. I just gave a summary, and saved the details for the next day. That Nivelles intermezzo was on the point to belong to the family's souvenirs. I would not return to that school for classes or for any things I had not brought in my suitcase.

The next morning, through the gendarmerie services, we alerted my parents, who were surprised and relieved by the news. Maman intended to come in two days, and we would happily wait for her. My four friends here were spread out in different schools in Namur, which were still open. Not for long. Grandpa's workshop had started to come alive again. What would come next?

Politiquer – Politisieren – Politicize

The politicians were back on stage. The King had been liberated by the Americans, but he and his family, previously transferred to Switzerland, were not home yet. Because of his past highly controversial attitude, his brother, the Prince Charles, became the Regent. Wait and see!

Back in Roisin, I found an effervescent place I never thought it could be. My H.Q. friends, like me, had changed a lot these past months, but there were still many flags to pin on our map. We remembered the time when, after a second thought, we didn't keep using our pins with the V, victory, as we considered them too dangerous if a "pro" visitor had seen them.

Busy, we ran all over. At the tram stop, we welcomed some former POWs arriving from Germany or comforted the families of those who would not come back. We could not get over the horror of the concentration camps. How could that exist? To believe it, we had to see the pictures and, more frightful, the shadowy appearance of some people we knew, coming back, one still in a striped outfit.

Dad had received a very welcoming return; still, the situation was not easy. Here too the last-minute

Resistance had arrested low-ranking pros and had killed a farmer who was the Black Legion chief's daughter's lover, but the chief was at large. So was our Herr Ober Something, Léon Degrelle's secretary. He probably had followed his boss who, a few weeks before, had flown to Spain.

Prison – Gefängnis – Prison

Dad was ensnaring his "game-birds," as he said. After the first plebeian rage passed, everyone went back to work. Trusting this fake peace, the wolves were coming out of the woods. Not long before they found themselves in jail.

One early morning, a man arrived full speed on his bike, panting, saying he had seen the Black Chief discreetly entering his home. Such imprudence didn't seem credible, but who knows? His family was still there. Discreetly too, Dad went with the ever-faithful Pélerin and they staked it out for a while. Sure enough, the guy came out from a neighbor's garden, dressed in civilian clothes, like someone going to work. He didn't go too far. The problem was to bring him to our little prison without arousing the village. No way! The tom-tom had already worked.

Everybody came out, they shouted, even tried to hurt the prisoner. A lady, whose husband was dying after his recent liberation from Dachau, came like a fury and, unexpectedly, planted a fork almost in the guy's eye. Dad stopped and said severely that he wanted the man alive to be judged and pay for his crimes. Being killed now would be too good for him. The argument worked out. Maman and I had noticed the uproar; we came out and, petrified, we saw the furious mob. Dad and Pélerin held the man, who was tinged with blood. The growing crowd, which had followed, had to stop at the courtyard door. The grammar school director insisted on showing the scene to his seventh graders as an example. Fortunately, the other pros were not as hated, and that sort of painful event didn't happen anymore. After the blown-up bridge, the mob's rage is what scared me the most.

Langue – Sprache – Language

Soon after came a panicky call from a farmer. He had a downed American plane on his field and a shook-up pilot in his kitchen. As my three-and-a-half English words could help, Dad took me along. The plane was a tiny observation plane. The young pilot had no apparent injuries, but one could see he was badly suffering from pain in his back. It seemed he didn't yet understand what had happened to him. He kept silent about his dog tag, his name, and the rest. He was on a mission and could not give any information. When he understood Dad was calling a doctor and an ambulance, he had an adverse reaction: "NO, not in a German hospital." Poor pilot, completely lost, he thought he had landed in Germany. We tried to reassure him, we showed him a map, explained he was in the Belgian freed part, but he kept a straight, doubtful face. Meanwhile, Dad had called the American H.Q. in Mons. Our pilot had a large relieved smile when he saw the American ambulance and heard his fellow citizens. Before leaving, he accepted the coffee the farmer's wife had prepared for him.

When he looked closely at the plane, the farmer exclaimed, "Look, part of its tail is in France!"

To avoid hair-splitting double international formalities, we all rapidly joined our energies and pushed back the lighter, litigious part onto Belgian territory.

Armée – Heer – Army

Instability in our country's organization was still rampant. General Eisenhower wished that Belgium would disarm the Resistance and reorganize its own army. This Army part was easy. Since the Liberation, five thousand men had already been trained in Ireland. They wore British uniforms. The funny Belgian soldier's cap, with a twitching tassel on the front, was definitely out of style. Many volunteers were still leaving for Ireland with this practical recommendation: don't kiss a girl or, her father or brother will consider the fact as a marriage proposal. Among the fifty thousand who went, I don't know how many did follow that advice.

To disarm the Resistance was not so simple. Some elements didn't agree with the conditions, and a few people were injured in a riot in Brussels, near the Parliament. Good that the "Supreme headquarters Allied Expeditionary Forces" still had some influence on the civilian side.

Monnaie – Geld – Money

When the Treasury Minister Camille Gutt changed our currency, he "put his foot in an anthill." Each person was allowed to exchange two thousand out-of-style war-time francs, plus receive new currency for ten percent of the funds they had declared before the war on 1940 taxes.

Panic among the dealers, they could not convert their war-time profits. They desperately tried to convince large families, who didn't have two thousand franks a person, to exchange funds for them. Rapidly placing the money in valuable objects was difficult, in the countryside the choice was sadly reduced, except for pianos. Many nice items had been destroyed during the war or were simply not being made. Apparently wartime had not allowed pianists to move or sell their treasure. In our area, the daughters of some farmers, largely provided by a profitable black market, had the possibility to be proud of showing what stayed, most of the time, a deluxe piece of furniture. Those girls never learned how to play pianos.

The rationing started to get better. The Allies gave us the leftover German food provision stocks. To go back to normal would take much longer. Agriculture, transportation, and business had to be seriously improved before all the ration tickets could be taken away. Rice and imported butter were the last food items still being rationed in 1948. The Allies were thankful for the Belgian Congo intense mobilization in the U.K. and the U.S.A. favor, they sent cobalt, tungsten, cotton, rubber, oil, diamonds, and, especially important — one thousand tons of uranium, secretly that was sent to the U.S. in 1940. Due to Uranium, which, later on would serve to make the atomic bomb, we were provided for than the French who had not been able to provide those special items.

We sent packages to the family and to our Réalmont friends. Coffee was their preferred item. Now Maman could enjoy her precious coffee again. At last, we had real soap, not that mixture partly made out of horse-chestnut, which produced a lot of unproductive foam. After the military toilet soap, impregnated with disinfectant, we enjoyed the normal one. I stop using the out of place barber's shaving cream sticks. I had used these past years, happy enough to get it from a friend who had a cousin-in-law who had a niece who knew a hairdresser.

For Christmas, now we would be able to bake a real cake, even with a little chocolaty decoration. V1 and V2 still sporadically fell on Antwerp. As they didn't seem to have more objectives in our area, we would have our first family Christmas party anyway. So Maman and I left for Havré to help prepare the reunion. Dad would come for the celebration.

Encore – Wieder – Again

The next morning we heard the worst news. Nobody expected the enormous German "Konigstigers" tanks to be able to attack us again, yet they were almost in Dinant, forty miles away. The weather was awful, low clouds, fog, and even snow in the Ardennes. Montgomery in the North and Patton in the South counterattacked with thousands of men, but without the help of planes, it was murder. While he investigated in Bastogne, General McAuliffe received a message from the Germans asking him to surrender. His answer became legendary—he simply answered: "NUTS."

The weather cleared up, and the Americans could parachute men and material into Bastogne. There and in the surroundings, the inhabitants, besides other help, gave their white sheets for the soldiers' camouflage. What destruction again! No use to say our family reunion and the victory cake had been forgotten. We spent that sad and frightful Christmas in prayers and brought back all war memories, even from W.W.I as its last casualty, an unlucky British soldier, had been killed in Havré on November 11, 1918.

December 26, Victory! Patton was in Bastogne, but the stubborn enemy tried to come back a few times. It took until January 17 to get rid of them. The Battle of the Bulge cost twenty thousand casualties; more than seventy thousand were injured or disappeared on both sides. Six hundred civilians in Malmédy were bombed by error. Now we were sure the Germans would not come back anymore.

Devoir – Pflicht – Duty

At home, Dad found his promotion: he would command a much larger brigade. He was also nominated for a succession of decorations. We were proud of him—he surely deserved them.

So, what to do while we waited for the departure to his new assignment? Find a school, a temporary one, of course. Because of my preceding school adventures, which seemed to influence the enemy's attention, my grandfather teased me saying, "Be careful, the Japanese are not out yet. Don't attract them over here."

I was not the only one in that situation. A school in Quiévrain opened a class. Nothing really serious, just enough to keep girls busy. They offered classes in drawing, sewing, and embroidery! Embroidery made me remember my first grade friend Renaud who did

Irène and Marcel (Dad) in the street - Dad re-incorporated

my work, a gardener watering tulips, in exchange for his math work. I wished he was here now to do my embroidery. Fortunately, the school had saved its nice library, so it was fun anyway. The modern tramway ran again, only four times a day, but with a better schedule. I could leave home at 7 a.m. instead of 6. Twice a week I would visit our cousins who lived near the school. Their son, Andre, was ready to leave for Ireland as a volunteer. His father was very busy readjusting to the new money business in the bank where he was the director. Cousin Simone was, as always, available to people who needed help. A nice, active family.

We still visited our friends who lived at the edge of the forest. They had no more news from the Jewish boy and his family gone back home. They didn't reopen the hotel section, rented now as a country-type restaurant. They just kept the private residence, which included the museum. Emile Verhaeren's spirit was now possibly disturbed by our jazz music. We loved to learn how to dance to our favorite, Glen Miller's Band.

Partager – Teilen – Divide

Through the radio, we were put back to the serious historical situation. In February, at the Yalta Conference, Roosevelt, Stalin, and Churchill discussed Germany's future and, by the way, demarcation of the occupation zones, pieces of territories that would be exchanged here and there. As the German goose was cooked, Stalin promised to help with taking care of the Japanese; he would declare war on them in August. Dad was doubtful about the future of that association. He trusted neither Stalin nor his politics and the brave President Roosevelt seemed so tired. Well, let's hope! Some people thought that only three partners was not a sufficient guaranty for the future when so many others had been so actively involved in the liberation process.

In March, the Allies were able to cross the Rhine in Germany, thanks to a German prisoner who, at the last minute, had alerted them that the Remagen Bridge was armed to blow up.

Deep sadness on April 12 when we learned that President Roosevelt had died of a cerebral hemorrhage in his residence in Georgia. He was loved and respected for being such a courageous and wise man. We didn't know his successor. We presumed that, chosen to assure the succession, Harry Truman had to be the right person. We were sorry Roosevelt would not see the end of this nightmare.

The Allies then progressed in the direction of Turgau where, at the end of April, they met the Russians. Every newspaper showed pictures of the event. Hesitation in our V flags placement. Patton had to stop his advance to Prague. To be politically correct, he had to let the Russians liberate Czechoslovakia. Prague resisted for over a week.

The end of April was sure filled with events. Italy got rid of Mussolini. He and his mistress, Clara Petacci, who had tried an escape to Switzerland, were shot by the Italian Resistance, their bodies exposed like slaughtered pigs. After his arrest, ordered by King Emmanuel III in 1943 and later saved by the Germans, Mussolini had founded the Italian Republic in Salo. This name, like the "Good Aryan" before, had become a phonetic joke. Salo, pronounced in French like "salaud," means bastard. The right word after all. Mussolini had killed all the fascists opposed to his regime, including his son-in-law, Ciano, who was his minister of foreign affairs.

Two days later, Hitler and his brand-new wife,

Eva Braun, committed suicide in their bunker in Berlin. One of Hitler's partners, Goebbels, did the same after he had poisoned his wife and their six children. Admiral Donitz then succeeded the Fuhrer. At the beginning of May, the Allies entered Munich, the French entered Bertchesgaden, and the Soviets entered Berlin.

Finir – Endigen – End

May 8, 1945: Cousin Simone was radiant when I came to their house after school. Germany had surrendered, the seventh in Reims, the eighth in Berlin. She and the other new volunteers' mothers could feel relaxed.

War was finished. Did that mean we would not hear air raid warnings anymore? No worry about V1 and V2, which had destroyed more than sixty-four thousand houses, killing six thousand Belgians and around nine hundred Allied soldiers. Would black leather coats, green and gray colors not give shivers anymore?

As exuberant as the Liberation had been, the announcement of the end of the conflict was sure a relief, but tarnished by the Far East situation. People were very thankful to the Americans who had liberated them and were friendly, with all the lively soldiers running around. So happiness could not be complete before it would be possible to rejoice all together.

When I came home, I found the whole brigade celebrating the event with my parents. I was a little puzzled to see my father not as enthusiastic as usual when foreseeing the post war.

Readjust to a normal life would take him long.

With my friends, we solemnly dissolved our childish H.Q., took our map off the wall, and burned it. We laughed with silly jokes. We pretended to scare each other with "ifs." If the last hidden V2 decided to fly by themselves, if . . .

The only living souvenir from our former German "occupant" was the last stable resident: the Russian horse, "Rossov."

Happy to have him the day I needed to go quickly to the hospital for a supposed appendicitis. No ambulance yet. As the surgery was not judged urgent, I had the "pleasure" of two rides, fifteen miles each, on paved roads in a carriage pulled by our Rossov. Not too moody that day, he stopped only once.

The POWs were progressively coming back. Our three French cousins, who had been married the same day in 1939, were home again. A Belgian cousin had been freed by some Russian soldiers who could not tell the difference between Belgian prisoners or German soldiers and had brashly stolen everybody's watch.

Gouvernement – Regierung – Government

Politically Belgium was trying to come back to life. As everybody wanted "everything right now," to establish priorities was difficult. The first government had already been replaced. It had only kept one "Londoner," Henry Spaak, a gifted and soon-successful European politician. The new and legendary Prime Minister Achille Van Acker (he came from the Flemish city of Bruges, so he pronounced it "Assil") had the most radical solution to the problems. The day the Postal Service had started a strike, he had decided the immediate dissolution of the whole postal service, and reopened it the next day with more cooperative workers. When asked about his rapid strategy, he said, "J'agis puis je réfléchis" ("I act and then I think)", an expression that Maman adopted when she made a mistake when knitting too fast. Later on, when the coal mine production was reorganized, his nickname became Assil Sarbon—for charbon (coal).

CHAPTER TEN

Peace

Transfert – Verlegung – Transfer

Another important day was when Dad received his transfer to Aulnois, a more populated village also on the French border. His job would consist not only of the routine work, but also of the Paris-Brussels international Rail-Way control. We were happy— the place was right for him. With a Belgian father, a French mother, a bi-cultural education, and a former interesting job on the borders, Dad was not an "inland person." Maman was happy too, as we would be closer to her parents in Havré and her sister in Genly. Hard to believe, but my schooling problem would be solved. The school my parents had always planned for me, the Sacred Heart, would reopen in September in Mons, just half an hour away by regular train. I would not miss the bombed Nivelles. As we say in this case, "The pearls were getting strung."

Before we left Roisin, we still participated in a few ceremonies. The first one took place in the nearest French village where the Maginot Line had been active in the 1940 battles. Captain Baliffe and his men had fiercely blocked the road to the Germans until the tanks had massacred all of them.

Everybody was touched when all the officials,

the schools, and the martial music met around the WWI monument on which had been added the WWII casualties' names. The townspeople brought as many flowers as they could.

After, we had a few good-bye parties, one with our unforgettable pipe smoker, Jacques, his mother, and his sister Nelly. As Maman had unpacked a minimum from the former moves, prepare the new one didn't take long. We were soon ready to close a long and very rich chapter.

Différence – Verschiedenheit – Difference

The new house didn't have such high ceilings, but had one more room. The garden was smaller, no problem, no need for high production anymore and never, never another rabbit.

The scenery in Aulnois was not as gorgeous as in Roisin—no rocks, no river. The frontier straddling complications was visible here too; no house like Lodie's, but a complete street — part Belgium and part French. When shopping, people bought bread, wine, cheese, and meat in France and just crossed the street to buy poultry, greens, coffee, beer, and tobacco in Belgium. If they purchased normal amounts, the custom agents didn't interfere.

The inhabitants were different: a few more rich farmers and mostly civil servants of every kind made the atmosphere a little more snobby, but much more interesting in their diversity.

In Aulnois, we had wonderful neighbors: a very sociable mother and her two unmarried daughters. The youngest one, Rosa, was a farmer in her soul. She had a mini farm on their property: one cow, one

*Paternal grandparnets Ernestine (Marguerite-Marie) with kitten,
neighbor Madame Lavenne, Maman, Dad, Uncle Charles, Aunt
Monique, Neighbor Rosa, Irène, Grandpa Edmond*

calf, one pig, one goat, one dog, one cat, one rooster,
and a few hens. Her sister, whom we soon called Aunt
"Tante Rose," was the local grammar school director.
Her favorite hobby was traveling.

Near them, a sweet retired couple lived in a little
country-style house surrounded by a meticulously
renewed flower garden. It was a blessing, as the
postwar situation was far from quietness.

A camp had been open in Casteau, not far from
Mons; it held the pros arrested in the region. Dad
helped to fill the place, as some fugitives regularly
tried to come back hidden in the international trains.
The most delicate operation had been to discreetly

arrest one of the Princess Liliane's brothers.

A sad day at the train station. A French POW, who came out of a German camp, was killed, his head caught in a sliding door during the train maneuver. He was Alsatian. His mother and his wife came from Mulhouse for the burial. His brother had been killed in 1940 in the North, but they had not yet found out where. The funeral service took place in Blaregnies, the next village, where a military cemetery had been recently open. Before they left, the two ladies had a look at the other graves; on the same row, they found the brother. Unbelievable! We brought them home to help them to overcome the shock. They spoke a mixture of French and Alsatian.

An ex-POW who had learned a local German during his captivity helped them fill out the numerous needed papers. He was competent and compassionate; he had lost his young wife in the 1940 bombing in Cambrai, France. The ladies came back a few times. Three years later, the nice helper and the young widow got married. Destiny!

Incroyable – Unglaublich – Incredible

In the Far East, battles and bombings were still terrible. On February 16, the Americans landed on the Corregidor Island in the Philippines. Forty percent of the Japanese large cities were partly destroyed, and the end of this war could not be seen yet.

In August, when we visited my grandparents, we heard the incredible news. A single plane had dropped a single atomic bomb, which had pulverized Hiroshima, killing fifty thousand people at once. A new era was open, the scariest of all. First, people stayed incredulous. Soon after, they did agree that it was the only way to stop the war. They felt sorry for and sympathetic to President Truman, who had to take such a decision. How was the Enola Gay's pilot feeling?

Two days later, Russia honored its promise and declared war on Japan. The next day, Nagasaki and its thirty-five thousand inhabitants disappeared the same way Hiroshima had.

What a relief when the Missouri anchored in Tokyo, to welcome the authorities ready to sign the peace treaty.

SEPTEMBER 2, 1945. REJOICE!

The nightmare was finally over. The American soldiers quartered in the area had a pretty good time, largely helped by the locals. The M.P. had a busy night.

Ouf! – Au weh! – Phew!

After this so-long-unwanted delay, we started the celebration of our postponed family's birthdays. This time, we had the possibility of enjoying it without an afterthought. We could bake the cake with even a bit of real chocolate in the icing. We had missed the parties five times.

Dad had to fill more papers and answer more questions to establish the file of his activities during the war. Months later, he received the confirmation of his rights. He would have the back pay for his obligatory leave, but the two moves due to the Germans' order would not be reimbursed because that case had not been foreseen in the rules! For his work in the Resistance, he would get a quarterly rent of about thirty-five dollars. He would also be awarded with the most complete series of decorations Mother Country could confer, after paying for the medals. Abashed, Florian, the gardener, asked Dad, "What did they offer you?"

With a blank voice, Dad said, "Their esteem."

Reacting with his practical common sense, Florian added "Good, but their esteem, you can't eat it."

The matter would have been easier to admit if, the same week, the notorious local pro dealer had not been sent home, back from the Casteau camp. He had not been judged guilty enough and had immediately been resettled in his job and reimbursed for all his expenses.

Not too long after, Dad received a confidential file coming from "way up." It needed some information about the pro dealer's daughter, a ravishing beauty, who lived in Brussels and was, let's say, in touch, with the highest society level. That explained many things, but it definitely gave a serious kick to my confidence in justice.

Etudes – Studium – Education

At last, real school started. This one, incredibly more open-minded than the previous one, offered the expected program for the BAC, equivalent to the first year college, and something new, a business school was opened. We were many who had lost too much time and didn't favorably foresee a diploma requiring a minimum of five years in University. I forgot about pharmacy, for which I had studied Latin and Greek in anticipation. As I had also entertained thoughts of architecture, but girls were not yet admitted in that subject.

The only black point was that, as a private school, the exams had to be taken in Brussels through the frightfully strict Central Jury. Well, the atmosphere here was positive—no reason to let yourself get overly impressed. The school adopted a new style, and the rules were looser: no more uniforms, just proper behavior, skirts should cover the knee cap, and no make-up. Rules that had survived: wear a hat outside and inside make a reverence to every "Mother" you met. These so-called reverences soon lost the royalty pomp, they became a simple, fast knee-bending. As for the hat, the door-keep Sister stopped me many times as my bushy hair could hide the object.

On top of the necessary courses, I could take: ink sketching with Mother Scholastique a specialist in miniature and its opposite in dimension, theater scene decors. I took choir singing, comedy lessons, and practice with Mrs. Urbain, a partner of the "Théatre du Parc" in Brussels. Fascinating years.

The railway system was not yet perfect, but the rides were not unpleasant, as a likable group attended high schools and universities in Mons. No fear anymore, you could talk to anyone.

The city was still cleaning its debris up. Little by little the stores were reopening. Many GIs added life to the streets. Some bars had an "Off Limit" poster on their doors, The M.P was vigilant. Even so, another black market was born. Some wheeler-dealer GIs could provide: canned meat, chocolate, nylon stockings, and cigarettes in such quantity that the American authorities had noticed it. They had checked closer and found out that some railway convoys were regularly "losing" boxcars on their way.

The Zazou outfit style disappeared, replaced, for the boys, by equipment bought at the American Army supplies. The girls adopted the Montgomery beret and the Veronica Lake or June Allyson hairdos.

Territoire – Gebiet – Territory

The Germany occupation and the annexation of some countries were organized in Postdam.

Russia obtained Czechoslovakia and Eastern Prussia. Its army stayed implanted in East Europe considering Poland, Romania, and Bulgaria as satellites. Poland, biting into Germany, could push its border to the Oder River. Since its liberation in 1944, Alsace was back with France and the Eupen-Malmédy area with Belgium.

More POWs were on the way home. Some came back with a German wife, some found their girlfriend married to a GI. Some married their "war godmother," the girl who had adopted them and sent them letters and packages to their camp. The world was turning with a few squeaks, but was turning anyway.

Remplacer – Erzetsen – Replace

As the Gendarmerie in Mons was lacking officers, Dad was "asked" to take the function, if not the pay, of a colonel, just for a few months. Advantage? A car with chauffeur, needed for the inspection of every single brigade in his district. Dad started with visits to his former colleagues and acquaintances. That way, he knew exactly, on the spot, how everything was running. As he was known for his experience and diplomacy to solve borders problems, he was, once again, involved in a new border tracing. How not to remember Lodie! At night, we talked about her. Suddenly, Dad exclaimed: "Oh! My Austrian boundary!"

Maman and I looked at each other. What else was going on with that stone? Well, to help some parachuting for the Chain, he had simply moved that historical mark a few yards onto the French territory. That stone had been placed by the Austrians in 1714 when Belgium didn't exist yet as a kingdom but was part of the Netherlands, themselves under the Austrian sovereignty. To avoid diplomatic confusion, Dad went to put the stone back to its place.

It was in Roisin, so he went to see Lodie. The chauffeur prudently stayed in the car. Even if Lodie had a few more cats and a few more layers of dust around, she was still witty and aware of everything. They both had a good laugh remembering the Germans' visit, and she promised to be nicer in case of a new survey. She was touched and honored that Dad had kept her in mind. For the sake of the traditional hospitality, she, of course, offered a cup of real coffee. Puzzled, the chauffeur saw Dad slipping a clove in his mouth when coming out. It was a tip our old doctor did recommend to stop eventual germs.

Mémorable – Denkwurdig – Unforgettable

The memorial era started: streets, avenues, parks, schools were named: Eisenhower, Patton, McAuliffe, Mac Arthur, Montgomery, Churchill, Leclerc. Chamberlain simply gave his name to an umbrella and Eden to a rigid felt hat.

At the train station, Dad was busy welcoming the personalities who entered Belgium. I had two

Marcel (Dad) in Kempen in 1920, occupation after WWI

more military handshakes in my collection: Marshall Montgomery followed by General de Gaulle. Dad had to escort him from Aulnois to Mons, where an enormous crowd was waiting to acclaim him. Dad had always respected the General for the nerve he had to refuse defeat and work hard for the country's rebirth in spite of some hard opposition. Now, after the ride, he admired his cold sense of humor and a simplicity you didn't expect when considering his stiff military attitude, his height, and his reputation.

While inspecting a list of German prisoners transferred in the area, Dad suddenly saw a name and an address that rang a bell in his mind. That was the family's name and the place, Kempen, he had gone as an occupant after W.W.I, small world! He immediately called the POW. After filling the papers, he asked him: "Do you remember four Belgian soldiers carrying the Kaiser's photo into your garden?"

The man turned pale—he didn't know what to expect. Laughing, Dad told him.

"Don't worry, in remembrance of your parents' understanding, of you, young chocolate fan, and of your little sister Francesca's sweet smile, I'll give you some advice to shorten your detention: be a volunteer to work in a coal mine. As soon as the Belgian personnel return from their war efforts to those jobs as a thank you for your good will, you will be sent home."

So the thankful prisoner did. A few months later, we received a card with an invitation to Kempen, but we declined. It was not yet the right time to travel. Dad had no free time for vacation, he was much too busy with his job. Besides, everything was under reconstruction. The few open hotels were too expensive for most people who had spent their savings on everyday needs, and for so long. The rationing tickets were still in effect. Our beloved seashore was far from being safe for tourists — too many bunkers and too many mines yet to clear.

Retrouver – Wieder treffen – Meet again
The vacations were spent between families. These reunions had been postponed for many years. First, we made a visit to my paternal grandparents in Revin. How moving it was, after six years, to find them at the train station, fit and happy again. Surprisingly, they still had their car, a Peugeot. To avoid its requisition,

they had wisely dismantled it and hid the pieces in various places. The good old Peugeot had come back to life without any problem; they were proud of the success.

It took a long time to get to their place, as the nearest bridge had been blown up and replaced by a simple footbridge. Conversation subjects when we finally arrived were fusing from all directions, all feelings, all names mixed up: relief, family members, evacuation hosts, Pétain, Laval, Vichy, de Gaulle, Allies, the Chain, pros, antis, heroes, Jean Moulin, and more. Le Maquis here had left the frightening memory of its 140 young men tortured after they had dig their own grave. Uncle Charles had been hiding from the S.T.O; a German residence was not his cup of tea. As many young people, with prospects or career led astray, he was now calling his future in question.

Confort – Komfort – Comfort

The conversation went on to Brûly-de-Peshes. In May 1940, during the German invasion, a group of SS had burst into this remote, picturesque and quiet village in the Belgian Ardennes, invaded the place, and chased the 117 inhabitants away. Same plan for the twenty-seven villages and cities around. Why? Because that place had been picked to build a well named "Wolfschlucht" (Wolf's haunt) for Hitler and his headquarters.

For twelve days, fifteen hundred men from the Todt Organization had taken care of the remodeling, covered the roofs with colored bitumen, opened new roads, and converted the top of the church steeple into a water tower. Daily tankers would bring the water from the near cities of Couvin or Chimay. As life had to be pleasant for high ranking Germans, they had erected two Bavarian-style chalets, a style used even to paint the road signs. One chalet nearby the Fountain St. Meen, shaded by old oaks, was for Hitler and the second, further out, for Goering. Both residences were very close to their camouflaged solid bunkers. Of course, with D.C.A. (Défense Contre Avions) A A, Ack, Ack anti-aircraft canons around them for protection.

A landing place had been opened for Hitler's private plane. They had enlarged the limpid creek to serve as a basin for his baths and new discreet paths for his walks, and a rotunda had been added for the open air conferences. In the existent village, the "Café de la Fontaine" and its out buildings—stable and cow house—had become hotel, the chicken-coop turned into a hospital, and the chicken house into a hairdresser's. The Communal House had been used as a strategic- maps bureau with the telephone directly in touch with Berlin. Keitel had lived there, von Braustitch preferring the presbytery. The Press Chief Dr. Dietrich had chosen the Café. The barn renamed "Wolf's Palace" had sometimes seen Hitler pleased to watch movies praising his glorious army. The Italian Count Ciano had paid some visits. Ciano was Mussolini's son-in-law, later on executed when their political views had become different.

The weather as nice as the countryside, life was pleasant; victories engendered an euphoric morale. This happy family, and the 150 SS men at its service, enjoyed the place until the end of the conflict in France.

Later on, the abashed repatriated inhabitants

wisely took advantage of their newly planned territory. Paradoxically, the whole area, which had been organized for some victors, became the nest for the next victors. Historically recurrent "got-ya." It soon served as a "Maquis" and a relay to the Secret Army, fearlessly helped by the villagers and even a priest as chaplain. In Brûly-de-Pesches, the whole population had been active.

Now, historians and pacific tourists invade the place. The Führer's bunker is still and will stay there, also the Fountain St. Meen; the birds are chirping and the special small mushrooms, their red cup decorated with white dots, grow again at the edge of the forest, back in its majestic mantle.

At night, we had dinner with my Godfather Maurice, who had visited us in our exodus in Réalmont, his wife Madeleine, and little cousin Colette, who had already turned eight. We enjoyed ourselves and talked into the wee hours. One story was about our cousin Pierre in Regniowez. At the Liberation, he was in the village steeple, ringing the bells and hanging an American flag, when a German tank division, escaped through this remote road, shot at him, fortunately missing their target. He was lucky they were in a rush; in some other villages they had taken the time to turn their guns and blow the whole church up. After all that had tragically happened, we considered ourselves as a well-protected family. People were thankful to the liberators and now to Adenauer, de Gaulle, and their courageous followers who wanted to build a peace bridge between France and Germany instead of the former mutual spirit of revenge.

Our trip to Douai was touching too, even though

we all missed Aunt Victoria. Marguerite and Aunt Boka were fine, but they were sorry not to offer us more lodging than the mansards. They had given a complete floor to a couple whose house had been demolished in a bombing. The École Normale had restarted, Normale in its name if not yet in its completely normal run, said Marguerite.

Travail – Arbeit – Work

At last, his colonel part finished, Dad was back in Aulnois. Soon after, a ceremony had been organized in memory of the former officer Wilmet, executed during the war. The local VIPs, and the officers from Mons came and put a commemorative marble plaque on the building. After Dad had received his first "load" of decorations, my parents gave a memorable party for the French and Belgian officers who had supported him in his actions. The most important were the Belgian Colonel Remy and the French Colonel Jaminet, who specially came from the Pyrenees. Their wives and some friends were included in the Memorial Day. Maman had made a buffet with what was on board and baked numerous fruit tarts, brown sugar tarts (a Belgian specialty), and more. She had not lost her hand—her delicacies were most appreciated. We had much fun and, no leftovers. Dad received official congratulations in the mail and was honored by some articles in newspapers and magazines.

Procès – Rechtsgang – Trial

The Nuremberg trial started. Twenty-eight personalities and eight Nazi organizations were facing it. It was attentively followed everywhere; how and when would that nuisance be eradicated? Trials started here too. Surprisingly swiftly "de-Nazified," some former pros had already almost no recollection of fascism. Some dealers were still dealing and would stay dealers, just a question of effective partnership.

Back in the routine, the first arrest Dad had to make was rather delicate, far from expected. He had to arrest the village priest, in his sixties, who had an ambiguous relationship with some local children. A revolution!

Nouveau – Neu – New

Another revolution was incubating: the "Royal Question." The Flemish part of Belgium became the favorite of the Germans, it left a bitter reminder in the Walloon part. Some Flemish even wanted to become part of Germany. In 1940 Flemish refugees were allowed to return home before the Walloon refugees; Flemish soldiers were allowed to return home, but Walloon soldiers remained POWs. Now, chiefly for the paradoxical group: leftists – wanting to get rid of the monarchy plus part of the high society – not wanting a commoner, acted to block the King's return. The King's wife and all his in-laws being pro-German and also a notorious, plebeian Flemish family presented an obstacle to his return.

In the gendarmerie, a new general had been nominated in Brussels. He was so rigid that he had been nicknamed "The Robot." He had the reputation of being sneaky, and he already had got a few officers in trouble. In fact, he arrived once around 12 a.m. Dad was just going to bed when he heard that a car was stopping at a distance from the front door. From the hall window, he saw two men in civilian costumes; they came one on each side of the door, and a third one was already ringing the bell, shouting, "What takes you so long?"

The orderly had to cross the front yard. As soon as he understood who the visitors were, Dad attracted his attention and made a gesture that could mean "Robot," so the welcome would be formal enough. Soon after, Dad came out in his impeccable uniform to introduce himself according to the correct formula. Taken aback, the general asked, "What are you doing fully dressed at this time?"

"My General, I was going to a surprise inspection at the night train control. As it must interest you, I will indicate the way to your chauffeur."

Pleased, the general invited Dad to accompany them, but he said, "Thank you my General, but it's much better if I go on my bike as usual."

Needless to say, the chauffeur was given the longest country road possible, and Dad whizzed to the station by the shortest. When the inspectors arrived, Dad formally introduced the four irreproachable men on duty. He also adroitly praised the good old bike, which made the transportation quicker in a village. The general thus impressed, maybe a little suspicious, seemed satisfied. That remained the only visit he made to Aulnois. For the first time, The Robot had been tricked. Later on we read that story of the Robot being duped by father in a magazine.

Sentence – Urteil – Sentence

October 1, 1946: The International American-British-French-Russian Military Court gave the verdict in the Nuremberg trial. Nobody missed a single detail:

The eight Nazi organizations were convicted of being criminal. The personalities: Goering, von Ribbentrop, Franck, Frick, Streicher, Sauckel, Seys-Inquat, Kaltenbrunnen, and Keitel were sentenced to death. They would be hanged on the 16th, except Goering, who committed suicide to avoid the execution.

Hess, Funk, and Raeder were sentenced to life in prison. Speer and von Shirach to twenty years, von Neurath to fifteen, and Donitz to ten. Schacht, Fritsch, and von Papen were discharged. Justice was done.

In 1948, in Tokyo and the Far East, five thousand Japanese were sentenced. The Emperor Hiro-hito was pardoned. We heard the coal miner, who traveled with us on our way to school, giving this comment: "C'est toudi les p'tits qu'on spotche" ("It's always the little people who are squashed.")

In Belgium, the courts showed some laxity. Léon Degrelle, escaped in Spain, was giving some interviews from there and nobody seemed to care. His secretary, our dear Herr Ober Something, had completely disappeared. Van de Wiele who had been nominated by the Germans as "Fuhrer for the Committee of Flemish Liberation," as he and his partisans wanted to be attached to the Great Reich, were sentenced to death but not executed. Belgium did not have the death penalty except for war crimes or high treason but did not use that option.

In 1963, Van de Wiele went to live in Germany. The Historian Hendrick Elias, from Ghent, was sentenced to death, but liberated in 1959 for health reasons! He quietly died in 1979. But some pros were sentenced to be shot to death and were shot, some others had long terms in prison. We heard that our Black Legion Chief had been considered a recruiter not a murderer. By that time, my father didn't want to hear anything about war. We tried to ignore the rest of the story. Now, every layer of the society would judge its members or better its opponents, sometimes just pick a quarrel with writers or artists who had kept working even without a Nazi orientation.

War wreckages' smoky smell was still floating in the air that, when the values courageous people fought for, were already being veiled by profitable horse trading and sacrifices falling into suitable oblivion.

The fact of growing up through the war and the after-war effects deeply marked me and left a definitive opinion about a few facts:

1- To use God's name in a patriotic motto is an insult to God when it covers up arrogance, domination, and, so often, no defensible interests.

2- Citizens don't ask enough "WHY?" Maybe afraid to face a disturbing answer?

3- The recipe for turning people against each other is very simple: a dose of worries, a dose of pride, a convincing voice, a few flag-wavers of any kind and the sauce can thicken. A poet can be turned into a murderer.

Even if our nervous system could take a break, solid basic faith and love helped our family to adjust to the new era. It took a lot of goodwill, optimism, and forgiveness.

Soulagement – Erleichterung – Relief

Meanwhile, the great Marshall Plan brought a serious relief. All these war damages would be repaired much faster. It was an enormous help, a heavy weight off the people's shoulders as much as another reason to be thankful. In 1947, the creation of BENELUX, a customs union between Belgium, the Netherlands, and Luxembourg, started a difficult economic rally.

Restauration – Wieder auf den Thron setzen – Restoration

The solution to the King's problem? The government finally decided to have a referendum to find out if the King could come back from Switzerland or not. The result came slightly in his favor. The Regent Prince Charles could retire.

Léopold III and his family came back in 1950, to a rather hostile atmosphere. No leave for Dad at the time, the security services were constantly on alert. Mixing all economic and political dissatisfactions, it didn't take long before the country plunged into deep trouble: strikes and riots popped up until three participants were killed. Then the King abdicated in favor of his oldest son Baudouin, a twenty-one year old nice and shy prince who didn't seem to understand what his father had done wrong, but was going to devote himself to the country, which he did.

On July 17, 1951, on his coronation day, in the traditional army general's uniform, he looked so frail that the whole country was moved. Looking at his deep-set kepi (forage cap), my Walloon spirited Grandpa benevolently said, "Vo diri qu'on li a mis l' casquette du Grand Fernand." (You could think they put the Grand Fernand's cap on him.) The Tall

Fernand was the local road man who always wore a cap two sizes too large.

July 21, the National day, brought back the most welcomed calm.

Panoplie – Palette – Display

By then, Dad had received the following medals:

1. Palmes d'or Ordre de la Couronne,
2. Médaille d'or de l'Ordre de Léopold II.
3. Médaille Militaire de 1re Classe.
4. Médaille de la Résistance.
5. Médaille de la Guerre 1940-1945.
6. Croix de Guerre 1940-1945.
7. Chevalier de l'Ordre de Léopold.
8. Chevalier de l'Ordre de la Couronne.
9. Médaille du Militaire Combattant de la guerre 1940-1945.
10. Médaille du Volontaire de Guerre Combattant 1940-1945.
11. Médaille du Règne du Roi Albert 1er. This one received 11-25-1973 is the most prestigious.

On his side, Grandpa Arnold was honored with a National medal for having apprenticed the highest number of exceptional sculptors on wood during his woodwork career.

At the ceremony in Brussels, the new King attracted even more sympathy when he acted like a sensible young man instead of a traditional symbolic ornament. In the largest theater, from a throne on the scene, he saluted the different recipients in honor that a chamberlain was presenting one by one.

My father's medals

The audience congratulated every one with sincere applause. Suddenly, a shy, eldery participant, strapped up in what seemed like his long-ago wedding suit, and obviously at his first royal event, stopped at the foot of the dais, genuflected unexpectedly, and stretched out his hand for a hand shake. Immediately the King ran down, shook his hand, and gently talked to him. The whole theater gave them an extra round of warm applause. Back on his chair, the young King discreetly sled his kepi deeper on his forehead, but for a while, he couldn't conceal the laugh revealed by the slight up and down heaving of his shoulders.

Piège – Falle – Trap

Before closing the chapter of my wartime scholastic adventures comes my part in a foreign historical episode. Our war was over, but far away, a dangerous situation was the creation of the not-yet-recognized nation of Israel. Long difficult negotiations were going on that inspired highly criminal actions. The attackers chiefly aimed at Great Britain, which still held its mandate over Palestine. Letter bombs were addressed to personalities, and exploded when they reached their targets with expected result. The question was: how to stop the channels? This was a problem my father had on his agenda as he commanded the brigade special checking the border traffic at the brand-new Aulnois International train station. During that time, suspicious travelers attempted to cross the lines, and the express Paris-Bruxelles was a rapid and discreet way to travel.

What Dad called "my clients" was an amalgam of persons considered "non-grata" and expelled from the country. Citizens who seemed to forget their Justice Ban, court sentences, and tried to get in or out. Sometimes exiled persons tried to return, and sometimes people fleeing from sentences tried to sneak out. Remorseless pro Nazis who tried to visit family and friends, people traveling on false identification, and simply people who exercised non-authorized professions—all fell under my Dad's watchful eye.

Belgium expelled the French delinquents and France gave back the Belgians. Dad's work was also the business of international outlaws, passengers who carried contraband. At the border, the gendarmes and custom agents went through each train exercising "Control," looking for irregularities. Persons caught up by the control, every category was given to its respective affair's department. Until 1948, as some food rationing was still in use, smugglers of any kind were dropped into the Customs Services' hands. Some of those caught stayed in the custody of local magistrates, while some were taken by the diplomatic service.

Aulnois, Belgium gendarmerie where the said Elizabeth Lazarus was arrested in 1947

One morning Dad received the disturbing information that some Jewish persons seen in Belgium were personally transporting some of these famous explosive letter bombs to Paris. No detail about them, as communication was simple at that time. So Dad needed to keep a close eye on the arriving trains that were embarking on the three-hour ride to the French capital. Dad decided to quickly stretch a trap here at the border, at the intervening stops, and at the Paris Gare du Nord.

It was June 1947, I was actively preparing for my next day redoubtable Jury Central exams in Brussels. I had worked hard and had been accepted to put two exams together.

This current case did not affect us too much, Dad had already solved so many delicate cases, even the discreet arrest of the former king's brother-in-law. I would have to spend two nights in a Brussels catholic boarding school used as a youth hotel, so I was packing my suitcase.

A group of undesirable travelers entered the courtyard. Among some "demoiselles" rounded up, one young girl seemed more attentive to the process. I thought that she had specially attracted my father's attention when I saw her enter the main office. From my second floor window, I had a view on that building. Curious, I picked the good view angle, they were talking seriously, peacefully. I saw her "client" state sliding into the "parishioner" when Dad escorted her into his private office, the one he called my Confessional Box. His assistant started to type, so I knew something special was up. Could she be one of these persons? She was. Dad shortly came home with a strange gleam in the eyes. He told me, "I could need you."

It had taken a long time for the girl to admit the fact. She had first given an explanation for the blank letters hidden in her bag. It was to help some stamp collector friends who liked to have some of their letters mailed in Paris. When Dad had gently said that, because of the current situation, his duty was to open them, she had not moved. Aiming a blade at a letter made her jump, screaming "Non!" She knew what she was carrying. Then she bravely finished the confession. She was supposed to meet a man at the Paris station. They didn't know each other, but he would recognize her by this funny hat she would wear, still tucked in her bag. Dad had already sent the information to Paris and here he was suggesting that I be the bait to spring the trap and catch her co-conspirator: "I will put an extra guard at distance. The French Police are already discreetly spread on the platform, would you like to wear this funny bibi in Paris?"

How tempting for me!

The best articulated "NON!" crossed the room. It came from my mother, who brought us back to reality. "And who is going to lose a year and the confidence of the Jury, when postponing the specially accepted exams at the last minute? For what reason? In this case for a confidential event with no risk of publicity admitted."

Maman was right. Anyway, now that the alert had been done and received along the length of the ride, perhaps the supplementary imposter became an unnecessary risk.

Pensive, I finished packing. But this tickling sense of human duty, scratching the heart, needed reflexion. Not so long ago, I had thought: Adventure of that kind? I would have been a willing bait for the trap. I hoped that this extension of the wartime tactics would end and be no more. It was not the political issue that concerned me, but the method—killing people because they had a different view, not because they were committing atrocities.

The suspected waiting man in Paris didn't notice he was followed by fake civilians, who harvested precious details along the way, and later on they escorted him to a comfy police van. On our side, the arrested girl and the confiscated, carefully transported, letters were transferred to the diplomatic service, which was very interested in them. The curtain fell on the case of the young lady who called herself Elisabeth Lazarus, proud of her historical cause.

Dernier chapitre – Letztes Kapitel – Last chapter

I survived with success the Central Jury with an A in French, an A in business law, and I was chartered accountant. It nicely reassured my dear Grandpa, I mean without setting new conflicts off. He teased me that each time I entered a new school it seemed to trigger a new invasion. I could keep going on to new fields and go deeper in the subjects I was really interested in: sketch, paint, sing, act, and have a serious look on cooking, according to what was possible to do during that still-convalescent time. In between, Maman and Grandma would add the arts they were experts at: decoration, writing, with emphasis on orthography – in spite of the A which didn't convince them to have totally covered the subject. They thought my spelling required constant vigilance. They both added personal recipes and, on a more philosophical side, with Dad, they all showed me the way to take the best of what the wind could blow.

Progressively, life took care to spread in all directions the people we had been related to.

Because of studies or carriers, some went to the Congo, the Belgian colony in Africa. Family or health reasons, moves or retirements sent some on other ways.

We turned our thoughts toward normal banalities. Social life had popped up. I could attend official balls with, according to tradition, a chaperon, of course. It was still in style that my mother or even better, both parents, were highly recommended to attend with me. There, I could wear my first long dress that showed a bit or cleavage, my first pearl necklace and dance, dance.

Would I still meet the interesting French student with such dark brown eyes?

> History story
> stored in deep memory
> too deep to worry.
>   Are you sure?